D1365474

Tim Bascom clearly outlines the dimensions of cultural
imprisonment and tells from experience how
we may find spiritual freedom. Readers are in for a
liberating and affirming experience.

William W. Weidrich
Bishop Suffragan, Episcopal Diocese of Chicago

The Comfort Trap *will speak to the hearts of readers who find it
difficult to focus on Christ while living in a culture that offers so
many distractions and temptations. I highly recommend it.*

Robert Stickney
Director, HNGR Program, Wheaton College

*This book is a celebration of life in all of its fullness. Tim Bascom
has a unique gift of discerning truth in every aspect of life. He
culls wonderful lessons by observing nature, relationships, recrea-
tion, music, worship and the limitless little events of everyday life.
He is also an artist who can paint beautiful yet clear word pic-
tures. This book is a joy to read.*

David M. Howard
David C. Cook Foundation

THE COMFORT TRAP

Spiritual Dangers of the Convenience Culture

TIM BASCOM

INTERVARSITY PRESS
DOWNERS GROVE, ILLINOIS 60515

InterVarsity Press® is the book-publishing division of InterVarsity Christian Fellowship®, a student movement active on campus at hundreds of universities, colleges and schools of nursing in the United States of America, and a member movement of the International Fellowship of Evangelical Students. For information about local and regional activities, write Public Relations Dept., InterVarsity Christian Fellowship, 6400 Schroeder Rd., P.O. Box 7895, Madison, WI 53707-7895.

Cover photograph: Michael Goss
ISBN 0-8308-1658-5
Printed in the United States of America ∞

Library of Congress Cataloging-in-Publication Data

Bascom, Tim, 1961-
    The comfort trap: spiritual dangers of the convenience culture/
Tim Bascom.
    p.   cm.
    Includes bibliographical references.
    ISBN 0-8308-1658-5
    1. Christianity and culture. 2. Christian life—1960- 3. United
States—Moral conditions. 4. Bascom, Tim, 1961-   .   I. Title.
BR115.C8B38   1993
248.4—dc20
                                 93-27973
                                    CIP

17	16	15	14	13	12	11	10	9	8	7	6	5	4	3	2	1
06	05	04	03	02	01	00	99	98	97	96	95	94	93			

This book is dedicated to Cathy, who has helped me claim that I am a writer even when I doubted. What a gift, to be married to such a tireless and encouraging "editor."

Special thanks also to those wonderful friends who have believed in my writing: my lifelong soulmate Dan, Drew and Lynn, David and Marilyn, Mark and Karen. And I am not about to leave out my family: Mom, Dad, John and Nat. Thanks for all those years of support!

You can't hide it in a Volvo or a London Fog.
You can't hide it in a mansion with an imported dog.
No matter how we plan and rehearse
We're at a pink slip's mercy in a paper universe.
GREG BROWN, "JUST A BUM"

I woke, the dungeon flamed with light;
My chains fell off, my heart was free;
I rose, went forth, and followed thee.
CHARLES WESLEY, "AND CAN IT BE"

Preface

I love seven or eight American high-school kids. I'm not sure they know that. It's probably better they don't. If they did, I couldn't get near them. High-school kids aren't sure how to act when loved, particularly by someone older. Should they be respectfully obedient? Rebellious?

No, I am too old to be fully trusted. And so I must love them from a distance. Every Sunday. When they gather in our home as a youth group.

How attractive they are! Witty. Athletic. Vivacious. Full of intense hope and anger, sensitivity and fear. They almost glow with life, as if they carry something electric inside of them.

I spar with the guys, playing verbal hockey. They check me against the boards and leave me laughing.

I watch the girls gather, dancing from one place to another, full of secrets, and I am so entertained I could watch all day. They are a delight.

But then I am filled with dread. I catch one of them retreating into herself, scrunching down onto the couch, arms crossed, eyes lowered. Normally so talkative, today she says nothing. Why? Why should someone so vivacious suddenly be so withdrawn?

Or one of the guys avoids me, as if somehow I am trying to ruin his life. He hides from me and from the others, never fully joining the group. Why?

I want to help these brothers and sisters break free to live fully. Instead, on some days I watch helplessly as they choose to shrink—like butterflies going backward, *into* their cocoons. On those days I can almost see their budding life squeezed back into its shell, into a tiny box of teenage perspectives forced on them by their culture.

Out of all of those perspectives, the one that worries me most is this: that being Christian isn't relevant for modern people—that it is outdated. I can tell some days that they think Christianity isn't worth the time it takes to explore. They think it forces people to lead bland lives without reward, without adventure or joy or true meaning.

Nothing could be farther from the truth.

One of the kids I love wants more than anything to be beautiful.

For some odd reason, she thinks she must strive for beauty as if it is something that can be won. She spells it out: "I want to be beautiful—and rich—because our society seems to put a lot of emphasis on those two things."

Oh, so true. Her society, like other success-oriented ones, does put a lot of emphasis on those two things. But she is mistaken. If only she had the perspective of Christ rather than Madonna, she would know that she already *is* beautiful.

No, I'm not playing the let's-be-nice game. She isn't beautiful in that deep, hard-to-describe, just-a-little-overweight way. She is simply physically beautiful. But because of the way her culture is communicating to her, this wonderful girl can't see herself properly.

What I fear is that the light inside of her—the electricity of her youth—will be lost. Then, as with so many beautiful young people who die into adulthood, all that will remain of her self will be the shell, pretty at first glance but hollow, sad and ironically ugly.

If only she could see herself now as Christ does, she would stay beautiful forever. She would become even more beautiful. Christ doesn't turn people into toads. He takes all of us, even the ones who seem the least interesting, and turns us into royalty. If only we will let him, he will turn us all into beautiful and interesting and joyful people. He will help us be all that we can be.

I know this is true because I've watched Christ transforming some of the people closest to me: my wife, my parents, my brothers, many of my best friends. These people—the ones I admire most and whom I want to grow up to be like—all have something in common. They have let go of some popular assumptions of their culture. They have refused to shrink inside those small walls, boxing themselves into the tiny space called the U.S., or Canada, or Germany, or any of the other places where people supposedly lead lives of privilege.

Christ calls us to a much bigger place than the little house or neighborhood or nation we live in—to an incredibly open and rich place, so full of possibility that life never ceases to be exciting. He calls us into the vast kingdom of heaven, which stretches beyond every known and unknown galaxy into infinity, a kingdom which started before the first human civilization took shape and will continue into eternity long after the last civilization has crumbled, whether that be today's "Western" way of life or some new society waiting in the wings.

God calls us to join him in this wide open place, but it is not easy to arrive. It is not easy to be Christian in the affluent modern world. It is not easy to join the committed minority who live *against* the comfortable but powerful tide, swimming salmonlike, rebellious, countercultural.

It is never easy to be revolutionary. But it is challenging, and it is satisfying. And that is one more reason why being a Christian—being truly Christlike—is worthwhile.

That's what this book is all about. Trying to be like Christ in the First World.

One

Invisible Walls

I F I AM SO FREE AS AN AMERICAN CHRISTIAN, WHY DO I FEEL so trapped, so restless? And why do I struggle to stay alive spiritually?

For me, the wrestling has been constant and baffling. I have wondered if it was a personal quirk, like an inbuilt short circuit, but after talking with other Americans, I see it isn't. In fact, I see that people from other "Western" countries, and from modern cities worldwide, struggle as well. They wonder too: *If I'm free spiritually, what is holding me back?*

Wherever you are from, join me in the search for freedom. In my case, it began in Ethiopia, even before I was born.

Beacon on the Hill

In World War II, when the Italians invaded Ethiopia, a number of Protestant missionaries were evacuated out of Wallamo, a lush, mountainous area covered by rust-colored, sloping fields and groves of green eucalyptus. The missionaries left in distress. After years of effort, they had a handful of converts, but now it seemed their work was in vain. These simple farmers would surely fall back into spirit worship.

After the war the missionaries returned. To their amazement they found not a handful, but ten thousand Christians! The faith of those few had proven so strong, despite persecution by Italian soldiers, that the Wallamo tribe had been radically altered. Mount Damoto, the little grass-covered mountain near where the farmers lived, had become a mountain of faith, surrounded by new Christians; and the converts were rejoicing openly at the freedom Christ had brought them. At last they could stop sacrificing. They could walk safely by the big brooding trees and rocks where vengeful spirits had come out to torment any who did not show enough fear. They were loved and protected by God.

Twenty years passed. Then, in 1965, my family took up residence at the foot of Mount Damoto, as part of a new generation of missionaries. My father, a doctor, would work in the mission hospital. My mother would teach. I, only four then, would grow up alongside my two brothers.

One of my strongest memories from that time is seeing the mountain burned clear in preparation for the new planting season. That night we were eating at the home of the Klievers, who lived in the one mission house with a picture window. As we ate next to that window, we saw flames creep up the mountain in wiggling lines, then spread until they crowned the top in a great, leaping sheet of fire.

That's how I remember Mount Damoto. It was a beacon on a hill— the city of God that St. Augustine envisioned and that the Puritans hoped to build. It was lit by the very faith of the Christians who lived on it and around it.

Other strong associations go with that mountain, so big to my young eyes. Though it was verdant with life—a place for growing things—it was not always gentle. I remember my older brother John, my father and myself tearing our pants down and scraping madly at the fire ants that had attacked when we stood, unaware, on their seething trail. I remember also a path that passed along a steep precipice, and then a place where the path ended and I screamed, clinging to the thick grass, terrified for the first time of high places—places where one could fall and fall and fall.

But always, when we walked back down to our home, the farmers would greet us warmly as we passed. They would let us break off the chickpeas in their fields to nibble from the firm green pods, and they would send us on our way saying, "God be with you."

One of the patriarchs of that Christian community was still alive then. He would hike down from his home miles away and appear at our door, knocking softly. Others frightened me, but not Wandaro. I sensed his gentleness and his joy. His peppery hair covered the scars that remained from when Italian jailers, enraged by his fearless evangelism, had torn at his head. Some of his teeth were gone, kicked out by the same men, but I didn't notice that either, because he always smiled softly and warmly.

In Wandaro's hands was a small, thick book with homemade leather covers. It was a Bible in Amharic. This went everywhere with him. Indeed, when I saw Wandaro through the screen door, standing there with his wooden walking spear and a white shamma draped from his shoulders, it was as if he had stepped out of the pages of his precious Bible. He could just as well have been Abraham, or perhaps an old Paul on his last missionary journey.

I have not seen Wandaro since I was five, but he has traveled everywhere with me, still in his patriarchal robes, still carrying his Bible. And so has Mount Damoto, burning in the night, an emblem of true faith.

Where Did God Go?

Years passed and I *did* grow up, living on both sides of the Atlantic— in a small town in the United States and in several parts of East Africa. When I graduated from high school, we were stationed in Sudan. There, my childhood vision of Christianity had been reinforced by experiences with more African Christians—with people who had discovered that neither trouble nor hardship nor persecution nor famine nor nakedness nor danger nor sword could separate them from the love of God (Rom 8:35).

Then we returned to the United States and everything changed.

It would not be right to say that it changed overnight, as we flew through the darkness thirty thousand feet above the ocean. At boarding school in Kenya I had already become restless, asking difficult questions. Though I had shared in some of the suffering of Africans, I had also been protected from it by my white skin and my blue passport. I sensed I was a privileged person, and I could not rest easy in that knowledge. Oddly enough, I felt empty.

Back in the United States, my frustration intensified. As hard as I tried to communicate with God—to see God—I felt further and further cut off. I had returned to a "Christian" nation. I had freedom to worship as I pleased. But God seemed to recede in front of me, instead of getting closer. It was as if I were trying to run up the down escalator.

I was in college at the time, taking a religion course on the New Testament. While the professor explained Pentecost—all the rushing little flames and babble of unknown tongues—I stared out the window at a suburban winter landscape. The sky was a sheet of gray, hard and cold as frozen iron. The leafless branches along the streets were dark cracks in this uniform gray. There was no color left—just black pavement and white houses. Suddenly, in alarm, I realized that God might not exist. I could see and touch the hard trees outside. I could feel the shivering cold. But where was God? I couldn't sense his presence. Where had I gotten this ludicrous notion that there was some separate Being out there, imperceivable but real?

That same spring Kim died. A wonderful, vivacious classmate, Kim had become a friend because she shared a love of play. She was tall and big-boned, tended to skip instead of walk, and liked to make funny faces in public.

She had shocked me when she came to the cafeteria one morning with a smudge on her forehead. "Kim," I said, "you've got dirt on your forehead."

"That's not dirt," she replied, smirking at me. "It's ashes. Haven't you ever heard of Ash Wednesday?"

She explained, to my consternation, that she was Roman Catholic.

That worried me because I wasn't sure Catholics were saved. Raised Protestant, I'd always thought just the opposite. In fact, I had somehow gotten the impression that I should avoid Catholics altogether. Back in grade school in Kansas, I had gone around the block rather than walk in front of the Catholic church. It just seemed safer.

But I liked Kim. And despite that, one spring day she accidentally ran through a stop sign and disappeared off the face of this earth—simply disappeared. I couldn't fathom this. One day she was with us. The next, she was not.

I went walking in a late snow and stood under a street lamp watching the big white flakes materialize out of the dark. "Where is she?" I found myself asking, even shouting. "Where is she?" And I wasn't convinced anyone heard.

I had worried for Kim's soul, but now ironically my own felt lost. All the familiar points of reference that I had relied on as a child in Africa—the mountains of faith—were obscured. Partly, no doubt, that was because I was no longer a child and life had become more complex. But partly it was because I had left a place where spiritual reality was evident and important, and I had come to a place where it seemed simply irrelevant.

A Hopeless Pursuit

I remember that while we were still living in Wallamo, old Wandaro, who had suffered under the Italians, was honored to suffer again as Christ had suffered. He and several other men were taken to prison. When they were released, they walked back to their homes singing. They were not masochists. They just knew that they had been spiritually enlivened by this adversity. They could see life (and death) more clearly.

In the United States, by contrast, I have tended to feel trapped in a gray fog. Lacking day-to-day reminders here of the fragility of life,

I find that I easily fall victim to the dream of success and its sleepy gospel of fulfillment. And though I know there is more to life than the "pursuit of happiness," I am still seduced back into that pursuit, losing sight of Christ's ways.

We seek personal fulfillment in the U.S., but ironically our society produces unfulfilled people. Take, for instance, the character Dustin Hoffman plays in that sixties classic *The Graduate.*

I didn't watch that film until I was a safe thirty years old, partly because I had developed the impression as a child that it was pure poison. Friends of my parents—I overheard my mother say—had watched *The Graduate* and decided that they should try living out a free-love experiment, getting sex wherever they could. As you can guess, they ended up divorced.

Years later, with fear and trembling, I finally took from this Tree of the Knowledge of Good and Evil and ate. My reaction was nothing like that of my parents' friends. The film left me sad.

I remember in particular the opening scene. Here, if anywhere, is a young man who should be satisfied. High grades. Star athlete. Nice car. Business prospects. Everyone gathers to praise him on his graduation day, and what happens? He is forced into the swimming pool by his father—to demonstrate the scuba gear he's been given as a gift—and he hides on the bottom, completely alone, trapped in inexplicable misery.

As I watched, I found myself lying there too, breathing torturously from the air tank and looking up at the distorted figures of those milling around the pool. I too wanted to escape. Even though I had been spared much of the driven materialism and thoughtlessness from which this young man suffered, still I could feel it all around me, pumping in the veins of my society. And I had to agree with him: *Stay down there. Hide. This is not an easy place to be.*

Prison Without Walls

First-world societies like the U.S. are built on the premise that each of us has power to shape what happens to us. And to some extent, we do. Why, then, when we seem to succeed, are we still not happy? Why, then, does it seem doubly difficult to be Christian? After all, aren't we some of the most blessed Christians on the face of the earth? Given unlimited religious freedom? With endless resources?

It should be easy.

It's not.

It has taken me years to learn it, and to believe it, but being Christian in the convenience culture isn't easy. In fact, often being Christian in such a society is more difficult than being Christian where there is overt persecution. Wandaro at least knew when he was locked up. But we find ourselves imprisoned without knowing—caught in a prison without walls. On the surface we look and feel free. But internally we are lulled into captivity. It happens so gently, so insidiously, that we don't even see the prison walls.

Is there any escape? Are we doomed to leave our souls buried and to surface empty like Hoffman, the secular graduate, looking for nothing but personal gratification?

Thank God, no! The apostle's words are as true for us as they were for the Galatians two thousand years ago: "It is for freedom that Christ has set us free. Stand firm, then, and do not let yourselves be burdened again by a yoke of slavery" (Gal 5:1).

It is not easy to be a Christian in a society built on convenience, but I have learned that it is worth the effort. The Christians who really deal with life in such a setting go through each day fighting to stay alert to their culture, staying true to all that is good in it, resistant to everything else. Like the disciples in the garden of Gethsemane—that beautiful place where sleep came so easily and where betrayal lay waiting like a snake—they struggle to stay awake, watching with Christ. And when, with Christ's help and everlasting forgiveness, they succeed, they find a hard-earned freedom which is more satisfying than the freedom society dangles in front of them just out of reach. They discover, in living out an alternative lifestyle, that God *does* grant fulfillment, more fulfillment than they could have ever found in trying to live a Hollywood fantasy.

Although I may not be able to live Wandaro's life in my own country—because, to be practical, it does not demand such a life—I can learn from his example. I too can sing against my prison walls, even if they are unseen and dangerously comfortable. I can recognize those invisible walls for what they are. And recognizing them will be the first step toward breaking free.

Two

Prisoners of Freedom

ONE OF MY PERSONAL HEROES IS A MAN HARDLY ANYONE has ever heard of. I don't even remember his name. But ten years ago, he decided to fly. He got his hands on a bunch of weather balloons, tied them to a lawn chair and took off. All he carried with him was a soda and a BB gun.

He did this flight over Los Angeles, eventually getting so high he was blocking air traffic. In my mind's eye, I imagine him there, sitting back lazily in his aluminum chair, thousands of feet above a billowing cloud. He looks down through a gap in this bright white cloud, and he can see the bustling city, cars and trucks skittering down highways so distant that not a noise rises to him. The only sounds are his own breathing and the sudden spurt of the soda as he opens it.

This fellow toasts himself, the only man to have flown a lawn chair. Then a plane passes a half-mile away, and he waves. Inside, packed in with hundreds of other conventional travelers, a worried business-man sees him and sucks in his breath. *It's impossible. I can't be seeing what I'm seeing.* He says nothing, but wishes it *were* true. Wishes he were out there too, flying a lawn chair, completely free, no longer bound by his responsibilities: a job, a house, a church, a family.

The lawn-chair man is elated. *Forget the rules. Nobody can touch me now.* But occasionally he experiences a moment of panic. *What if one of the ropes snaps and the chair shifts? How long can I hang on? What if I drift over the ocean?*

He stays up for an hour. Then he lifts his BB gun and shoots one of the balloons. Nothing happens, so he shoots another balloon, and slowly, very slowly, he feels the chair descending. He waits a long time—it seems forever—before he shoots one more balloon. He doesn't want to drop too quickly.

The city grows under him, eventually making itself heard: the honk of a horn, the clatter of a train, a dog barking. And worries start to gather. *Where will I land? Will I miss the power lines?*

He looks down as he nears the ground and there are police cars. *How did they find out?* But he can't worry about them for long. He's headed toward some wires, then a tree. Whatever control he had is now gone. All he can do is pray. And he does.

Freedom Unlimited?

You'll be glad to know my hero made it down safely, although the Federal Aviation Administration immediately threatened to arrest him for violating air-traffic rules.[1] Such audacity! I practically applauded when I read the news. He actually flew a lawn chair.

In this country, we are rich with such free spirits. I'm sure they exist elsewhere, too; but in "the land of the free and the home of the brave," free spirits find fertile soil, take root and grow as big as Jack's magical beanstalk. "Be whatever you want to be," we say. "Just do your own thing."

I love the independence of such people and their wonderful eccentricities. I'm fascinated with people like Jeanette, the woman priest who has a black belt in karate, and Steve, who cross-country skied more than a thousand miles across Scandinavia, and the seventy-five-year-old construction worker I worked with who collected player pianos and made his own dandelion wine. Whatever these people are, they are not boring. They have color. And that's because they are free to do as they please.

The U.S. was built on such independence—"self-reliance," as Emerson called it in his famous essay.[2] Those who founded the New World had to be self-reliant to even think of leaving the Old World. And as their descendants—or the descendants of countless immigrants who have shown similar initiative—Americans are privileged to have inherited their way of looking at life.

Novelist Bharati Mukherjee, one of our more recent immigrants, would agree. She was the well-to-do daughter of an upper-class patriarch in India before she came to the U.S. to study. While she was at the University of Iowa, her parents wrote to say that they had found the perfect husband for her. Everything was arranged—the date, the dowry, the guests. All she had to do was to return and to marry. She realized at that moment that she never intended to go back. She stayed and married an American writer.

Mukherjee says, "What America offers me is romanticism and hope. I came out of a continent of cynicism and irony and despair. A traditional society where you are what you are, according to the family that you were born into, the caste, the class, the gender. Suddenly, I found myself in a country where—theoretically, anyway—merit counts, where I could . . . invent a whole new history for myself."[3]

Like her, I prize the freedom I experience in the United States and in other democratic Western societies. I have been in countries where you do only what the state allows, countries where you practically have to raise your hand to go to the bathroom—and then someone accompanies you. Such regimes have convinced me that I am blessed to belong to a *free* country.

But being free isn't always what it appears to be.

I Can Take Care of Myself!

Personally, I've had a history of being independent about my faith. For years I searched for a church that would do things the right way—my way. I tried the Pentecostal church, the Plymouth Brethren, the Christian and Missionary Alliance, the Evangelical Free, the all-black Baptist, the all-white Presbyterian, the sober Lutheran. Nothing satisfied me.

During the same time, a deep stubborn streak made me keep my thoughts to myself. I didn't want anyone to influence my decisions, sometimes not even God. I could take care of myself, thank you.

I consider it one of the supreme ironies of my life that I am now married to a minister. God was going to get me committed to a church, one way or the other! It's no surprise, either, that soon after Cathy and I were married I was approached by the director of the Sunday school at our church: "Tim, I was just wondering if . . ."

My immediate reaction: *Teach Sunday school? That's the last thing I want to do.* As far as I was concerned, Sunday school robbed kids of their right to think for themselves. Since I had overdosed on it as a child, Sunday school represented for me the worst kind of organized religion, a sort of saccharine brainwashing. And teaching would mean becoming part of that status quo system, becoming a Pharisee. Unthinkable.

So how did I respond? By jerking my fists into a boxer's stance?

No. To my surprise, I heard myself saying, "I guess I could teach. If you really need somebody."

I rationalized that I was saying yes because I could teach in a way that would allow kids to think. I figured I could protect their independence better than someone less "sensitive," less "enlightened." In any case, I was very rational about it all. But looking back, it wasn't a rational process at all. It usually isn't when the Holy Spirit is involved.

Someone's Knocking

I was given the eight-to-ten-year-old Sunday-school class. Since I had been tutoring Hispanic children the same age at a tutoring center in Chicago, I felt ready for them. If I could tutor children from gang-infested Logan Square, dealing with all their neuroses, then surely I could handle a group of tame suburban children. Right?

Wrong. I had never encountered children who were so unruly. No matter how firm or creative I was, by the end of every class I found myself in the middle of a caterwauling swirl of bunched-up construction paper, wrestling bodies and overturned glue bottles. They all competed remorselessly for attention, sometimes simply seeing who could shout or scream loudest. And they refused to cooperate with each other or me.

One of the most difficult moments came on the day we looked at the passage, "I stand at the door and knock. If anyone hears my voice and opens the door, I will come in and eat with him, and he with me" (Rev 3:20). I was ambivalent about this passage, so often used for evangelism. Were they old enough to think for themselves on such an important matter?

I asked if any of them had ever heard Christ knocking—if they had ever felt his presence waiting to be acknowledged.

Complete silence.

Then I tried to illustrate how that might happen—through the loving example of some Christian they respected, like their mother.

One of the oldest girls in the class, smart but equally sassy, shrugged. "Who cares about Jesus?" she blurted out. "I didn't ask him to come smashing down the door and intruding. He doesn't have any right to do that."

"Where does it say he smashes down doors?" I asked. "He stands at the door and knocks, that's all. Maybe he even knocks softly."

It hurt, listening to her. Here was Someone so loving that he would literally die to save us. He was gently knocking, and she wasn't willing to answer the door, let alone look through the peephole or ask, "Who is it? What do you want?"

A Right to Freedom?

Maybe her words drove home because I recognized in them the outrage of my own independence. Despite my odd transatlantic upbringing, I'm an archetypal Yankee, independent as can be. When I was a baby, according to legend I wouldn't let my mother hold me to nurse. I was always breaking away at a fast crawl, headed for the far side of the bed. When I was in grade school, if things weren't going my way, I used to slide under one of the beds at home and hide, completely alone in a musty world of bedspread, walls, mattress and lint-covered floor. I spent a lot of time down there, staring at the bed springs in a proud assertion of my right to do as I pleased—to be free—not unlike a prisoner staring at his bars. As the song goes, "I did it *my* way." But I didn't enjoy it.

So as I faced that stubborn, independent nine-year-old, I saw someone like myself—imprisoned by her own need for freedom. I saw someone needing to have Jesus come into her life, yet declaring, "He doesn't have any right to do that." I felt anger along with her, but anger at the way a good value can get twisted until it takes over and does us great damage.

Children will want their way no matter where they grow up. But I'm convinced that children here, unlike most, are actually *encouraged* to want their way—particularly middle-class white children. They inherit a Yankee spirit of independence almost as surely as they inherit the color of their eyes. And so one of the most deep-seated problems in our particular brand of Christianity is freedom run amuck. How can I speak the term *Lord* when I'm so fiercely determined to do as I please?

All in the Family

The Hispanic children I tutored in Chicago were very different from the white suburban kids I taught at our church. When I first visited the tutoring center, I envisioned them as gang-toughened loners with cynical smiles and razors in their pockets. Instead, I found them to be responsive and loving.

Regularly, when Cathy and I tracked down the cries of a child who had been hurt, we found an older child already there comforting the one in distress. Sometimes it was a brother or sister or cousin. But not always. They all treated each other like family, setting aside their own needs or goals to deal with others. They treated even us like family. On our arrival, the youngest ones would rush to us, calling out our names and hugging our legs in welcome. They were surprisingly well-adjusted, given the stresses of alienation in a foreign culture.

Why?

I believe it had to do with a mindset that is less driven toward independence, more accepting of outside forces and relationships. Their immigrant parents had passed on to them a way of seeing life that was less rigid. As a result, the kids didn't have to have everything their own way.

Like those Hispanic children, people in Africa and Asia and Latin America tend to be less hung up on preserving their own options. My experience in less developed countries (where I often lead workshops for writers) keeps reinforcing this hunch. People there hold to the wisdom of Proverbs: "In his heart a man plans his course, but the LORD determines his steps" (Prov 16:9). They don't see the need to be personally in control of all decisions. And they are freed up by surrendering this need.

Take the people of Ethiopia and Sudan. Those two countries nearly top the list as places without choices. They are hard places to live—even brutal. However, my father points out that, in his years there as a missionary doctor, he hardly ever had to treat anyone for stress-related diseases. In rural Africa he saw only two or three heart attacks, while in the U.S. heart attacks are the number one killer, even over cancer.

We're fed well, relatively speaking. And we are medically cared for. We live in luxury. So why all the heart trouble?

One of the key factors is stress. Apparently it's not easy having choices. After all, for every choice there is a corresponding decision!

Breaking Point

In the U.S. and other privileged societies, even small decisions can be stressful. There are 108 brands of cold cereal for me to choose from at our supermarket (I counted them).

Video shops are worse. I am lured into them by the prospect of spending a peaceful evening relaxing in front of a film. Instead, I waste hours spinning from shelf to shelf in feverish indecision.

Such decisions literally make us sick. In his groundbreaking book *Future Shock,* Alvin Toffler demonstrates that many of our modern illnesses are related directly to what he calls "decisional overstimulation." People dealing with a high level of change—and all the decisions that go with it—simply break down. The more difficult their decisions, the more fragile they become.[4]

Being Christian only makes it worse. Every decision has to be weighed not only on the grounds of personal desire but also on whether it fits with God's will. It's not enough to do the smart thing. Am I doing the *right* thing?

For those of us from the United States, this is all the more ironic, for it was because of Christian convictions that our citizens first insisted on the right to choose. The Pilgrims *chose* to come to America because they wanted freedom to *choose* their religion—their way of life. And with that as the model, we have become "The People of Choice."

Unlike the people of less democratic countries, which place less value on personal choice, we in the U.S. believe in choosing our own leaders, our careers, our spouses . . . and that's not all. Now our government is set up so that we can choose to divorce if that seems convenient. We can choose when to have a baby. We can even choose to get rid of a baby that's not yet born. (The latter are called "pro-choicers," by the way.) And all of this is integrally tied to the original desire to choose what we will believe—to worship freely.

I can't avoid the feeling of power that comes with this amazing freedom of choice. I may remind myself of what the Pilgrims always knew—that I still need God's guidance. But, unlike the Pilgrims, I live securely, in a stable, powerful nation. Why bother with God? I can take care of myself. Can't I?

The fact is, the more difficult my decisions become, the more stress I encounter. With choice comes the possibility of poor choice. Thus, I can have everything to choose from but still be unhappy. I can be like a friend who bought the latest model of a sports car—a sleek, expensive machine with no apparent flaws—but drove away dissatisfied. He couldn't help worrying that he could have gotten an even better car!

So we suffer—finite beings trying to be infinite like God. Impossible as it is, we believe in shaping destiny instead of being shaped by it.

A Lesson from the Muslims

I remember I used to become infuriated by the way the Sudanese accepted the limitations in their life. No matter what the problem, invariably someone would respond, "Maalesh," which means, in effect, "Oh well. It doesn't really matter." Then someone would add "Bukara," which means "Maybe tomorrow." And finally, "Inshallah." That is, "If God wills."

Maalesh. Bukara. Inshallah. Always this creed of fatalism.

Once I waited a full day in 110-degree heat to get gas from a gas-rationing line. After pushing the car down a creeping four-block row, trying to save the fuel left in the tank, I finally reached the front. Just then the pumps ran dry.

"Maalesh," the attendant said, shrugging his shoulders. "Bukara. Inshallah."

I wanted to scream. Then I realized he was right. The situation would matter only if I let it. Unless I accepted that fact, I would destroy myself with needless frustration.

In affluent, democratic societies, there are so many alternatives available that it's tempting to believe we actually control what happens. It may take a crisis to remind us that this is all an illusion. In reality, we are not in control. We had no choice about entering life, and in the end we'll have no choice about leaving it. Besides, no matter how much freedom God gives us, it is still a gift, not an achievement on our part. Only God (who gave us our opportunities) knows what is fully best for us.

The Sudanese believe in the goodness of God's guidance. That's why they say "Inshallah"—"If God wills, it will be." And although I may not be able to escape the decisions that go with being American, I can learn to look at them from this perspective. I can learn to include God in all my decisions.

To start with, I can pray.

Here Comes the King
If I want to restore God's involvement in my life, I find there is no substitute for prayer. Prayer is a direct acknowledgement of God's sovereignty. "Lord," I say, "May your kingdom come, not my own. Your will be done here on earth as it is in heaven." In prayer, I submit to the larger power and wisdom of God.

Of course, I have been schooled to think this is the worst form of compromise—to give up my own aims, my needs, my choice. So sometimes I cling stubbornly to my options. But when I let go, what a relief. In making one large decision—to trust God more than myself—I am set free from all the horrid mistakes that I am sure to make with smaller decisions when relying only on my desires. *I am set free from my very need for freedom.* Instead of living in anxiety, grasping for the control of my life like a lost driver who refuses all advice, I can sit back and relax, knowing that God knows the route even better than I. If I acknowledge him and listen to my own conscience, then God will direct my life safely into the future.

So I find it helpful to make submission a daily discipline. I try to start the day, before even rolling out of bed, by simply saying, "Lord, this is your day, not mine. Do with it what you will."

Try it the next time you find you've been living on your own wits. Stop to acknowledge God's sovereignty: "This is your day, God, not mine." The amazing thing is that when we do this, we can rest in the knowledge that God is at work, helping us to make right choices. There is freedom in knowing that the all-knowing and all-caring Creator is helping to give direction to what happens.

And although submission may seem antimodern or antidemocratic, it is purely Christian. Jesus came to do not his own will, but his Father's will. Likewise, I am asked to do not my will, but the will of Christ. As difficult as it is, I must learn to bow. Christ is my King, and wise people bow before royalty. When praying, I find that it doesn't hurt to literally bow, or to kneel, as a reminder of my relationship to Christ. Those postures began not as a way to concentrate, but as a way to acknowledge the Lord appropriately.

The good news is this: if we learn such submission, we learn the humility and flexibility to live in harmony with other people as well. We learn how to be liberated by our relationships rather than bound. And so, ironically, we *are* free!

Three

Free Love

I T WAS 6:30 A.M.—MUCH EARLIER THAN I GET UP, ESPECIALLY on a Sunday. And for two nights I had gone to bed late and gotten up early, exhausted. So I was not pleased to be wrenched out of deep slumber by a group of men bellowing hymns. I did not find it humorous that one of them was wearing a pink shower cap and rainbow suspenders. And it did not placate me that they were offering coffee and sweet rolls. If I had *asked* to eat breakfast at 6:30 with a barbershop quartet and a clown, fine. But as far as I was concerned, this was no better than a forced march in boot camp.

Although I was on a weekend spiritual retreat, at this point all hopes of spiritual growth vanished. "No, I don't want coffee," I muttered. "And no, I don't want to get up yet."

The others in the dorm were laughing it off, wandering blurry-eyed with coffee cups, like beggars in underwear. I watched awhile, then rolled out of bed determined to escape. I disappeared to the showers, hoping the rest would stay with their sweet rolls. And once out of the shower, I dressed quickly, saying nothing, then walked out of the building. *Okay, they want to surprise me. Then I'll surprise them. Forget the morning service. Forget breakfast. Forget stripping my bed. I don't need this.*

I didn't go back for two hours. In a nearby deserted park, I lay down on top of a cement wall. Slowly I gathered my thoughts, feeling the rising sun against my arms and face, hearing the birds chatter in a nearby cottonwood, watching a groundhog lumber out of his hole to forage for food. *Why is it so difficult to get along with other people?* I wondered.

The weekend had been good. The little community that had formed was full of thoughtful, caring men. But now they seemed like guards rather than friends. I couldn't seem to escape except like this, full of bitterness, misunderstood, feeling guilty for not being more cheerful or compliant. Why?

I looked across the park and saw my fellow spiritual sojourners coming out of the dorm, each carrying a pillowcase full of laundry. They looked a bit like members of some strange religious order that demanded that all earthly belongings fit into a single white bag. After they had dropped their laundry, they went to the dining hall, but I stayed on the wall, still watching, still not ready to be part of the group. Only when they had finished breakfast did I follow.

By the time I got to the dorm, they were leaving for the next meditation. I hadn't stripped my bed or packed, so I went to work. Then, unfortunately, one of the retreat directors found me. Bill was a huge, red-faced, white-haired retiree whose stomach bulged out between the bottom of his T-shirt and the belt of his pants. He wheezed a lot and hung around grinning and directing traffic. I knew what he was going to say before it even left his lips: "Hurry up, Tim. We can't start until everyone is there."

I thought I had found my internal peace by breaking away, but now feelings stormed up inside of me so violently I had to forcibly swallow them back. *They don't need me to start. They can do whatever they want, and it won't matter one bit if I am there.*

"I'm coming," I said. But Bill stood there while I kept packing, waiting as if I were a truant soldier who might go AWOL. As I shouldered my bag and walked past, ignoring him, he reached out and put his hand on my shoulder, pressing me toward the stairs. He had done this to me before, and I had watched him do it to others all weekend. I resented it—this paternal gesture, this corralling motion. Now I reached my limit. I swept his hand away and hissed, "Quit pushing me around. If I'd wanted to be in the army, I would have signed up."

The arrow shot home; Bill walked away.

As I stepped into the meeting room, where all the men were singing, their voices lifted triumphantly, I was full of bitterness. I could not join the worship feeling this way. A wall had formed between me and all of them. In rejecting one person, I had rejected all.

I stood there tight-lipped while they sang of Jesus' love, like Judas facing the other disciples. And that is when I realized my own need to repent. Regardless of how self-righteous I felt about being pushed around, my attitude was cutting me off from everyone. It was my problem, not theirs. I just wanted to *have everything my way.* And as a result I was forcing myself into a sort of solitary confinement.

When we had finished the meeting I went right to Bill. I put my hand on his shoulder. He turned, looking surprised, almost wary. And I said, "I'm sorry. I shouldn't have gotten so angry. There were other things bothering me."

It was amazing what that little gesture did for me. Without it, I would have remained removed from the whole group. But suddenly I was able to enjoy being with people. Before, I couldn't hear anything that was said. It was almost as if I had been put in a soundproof box. But after deciding to reach out and accept this one man, I was able to accept others. I could hear their voices again. In fact, Bill was the next speaker, and as I listened to him, I found myself reversing my whole impression of him. He became an intelligent, caring person, someone who was trying his best to live like Christ. And I realized that what I had found so annoying about him had actually been his attempt to show love. I even had to admit that maybe the clown with the sweet rolls had been trying to show love too.

Life on the Deserted Island

My problem on the weekend retreat was that I wanted to be in control of everything—even the way I was loved. But God taught me to let go—to appreciate others even when they introduced the unexpected. What an important lesson. It was either that or ignore every opportunity for friendship and live as if I were on a deserted island.

The fact is, it is *easy* to live as if I were on a deserted island. Stand next to any busy road in an affluent country, and you will see what I mean. Almost every car that passes has only one passenger. We are trained to function in our own sealed worlds, each of us shuttling back and forth with separate goals.

Even when we play, we do it more separately. Take basketball. It always has been a source of amusement to me, and of not a little frustration, to play basketball. I love basketball. It is a quintessentially American game, a game full of precise movements and dramatic contests. But the way it is played can bring out the darkest strains of individualism.

When I walk into the local gym to join a pickup game, I am sometimes struck by how aloof and competitive everyone is. Even the people on my own team are likely to treat me coolly. I used to wonder if there was something wrong with me—perhaps the way I cut my hair or the fact that I didn't wear high-top tennis shoes. But as I looked around, I saw that everyone else seemed just as cut off as I. Conversation was a rare thing, preserved only for those who knew each other well. And even then there was a keyed-up intensity to every interaction.

I went to play ball at one gym for six months, always with the same group of men, and I found it virtually impossible to get to know any of them. They treated the game like a job—something to do quickly so that they could go on to something else.

I also like to play soccer. To play soccer in Chicago means to play with people from other cultures, often Latin Americans. The contrast is remarkable. Even though I am white, I am welcomed onto the field with handshakes. The men introduce themselves. There is a lot of joking and laughter during the game. And when it is over, someone typically buys drinks for the whole group. They flop down on the grass to talk, and they often invite me to sit with them, translating for me in broken English what is being said.

The Hispanic soccer players may not always show up on time for the game. They aren't nearly as time-efficient as most basketball players. But they see the sport as much more than a private proving ground. It is a place to develop friendships, to experience community.

Now, what has all this to do with Christianity in individualistic societies? A lot. The same spirit of isolation that is present in the sporting arena is carried everywhere else—even into the church. For culture is not a coat we can take off and leave at the door.

A Very "Independent" Church

Take, for example, a popular church in the Chicago area—one which could be classified as "independent," like so many churches today. It holds thousands for each of its Sunday-morning services. The congregation meets in a huge auditorium with one wall that is nothing but glass, opening out on rolling fields. The floor ascends from a stage at front, and the congregation sits in sections of plush fold-down seats like the ones in a movie theater.

When I enter that church, there is the feeling that something exciting is going to happen—a real event. Why else would so many have gathered? I look around to find somebody I know, and I recognize one or two familiar faces in the huge crowd. I can only wave since there are so many people in the aisles. I sit down and wait for the action to begin, and when it does, I am not disappointed. The service is full of well-rehearsed performances by musical ensembles and drama groups. The sermon is dynamic, delivered like lines from a play. I walk out, feeling lucky to get all this for free, a bit as if I'd been to a very good benefit concert. Outside, I spend fifteen minutes in my car, creeping past a battalion of baton-waving volunteers and police who unload the parking lot as they would after a championship basketball game. This is a thriving, successful church.

So why don't I feel comfortable there?

I once asked an acquaintance who is a long-time member there why that church has grown so large. He replied, "Because it puts no obligations on anyone. I can be perfectly anonymous."

I honestly hope that he is wrong. I happen to know that the founders who started this church used careful research to shape it. They were aware that lots of suburban Chicagoans would be attracted to a place where they could explore Christianity at a safe distance, free of obligation. And, to their credit, they shaped the church so that there are higher levels of involvement and smaller, more personal groups which people can choose to pursue. They want to draw in the uninitiated, then to involve them more fully. In that sense, they are doing the best thing a church could do—drawing in the wary ones.

But I have often wondered how many of these churchgoers, like my acquaintance, never go deeper than the one service every Sunday morning, slipping in and out anonymously before going home to the unencumbered privacy of their homes. I have feared he was right about the reason many people attend there. Such Christianity is comfortable. It's convenient. It can even be entertaining. But it is not Christlike. And, in that sense, it is a trap.

The Love Choice

When asked which commandment was the greatest, Christ answered, " 'Love the Lord your God with all your heart and with all your soul and with all your mind.' This is the first and greatest commandment. And the second is like it: 'Love your neighbor as yourself' " (Mt 22:37-39). He answered with two commandments instead of one because the two were inseparable. It is impossible for me to love God without loving my neighbor as myself. As Jesus explained, when talking about his eventual return, "Whatever you did for one of the least of these brothers of mine, you did for me" (Mt 25:40).

Christ was always showing interest and respect for others, and often for the least likely people. He stopped for children, for blind men, for lepers, for demoniacs.

The odd thing is that it's hard to make progress in the company of such people. They hold you back. But Christ wasn't progressive, not in the Western sense of the word. If anyone could stand alone, without any outside help, it was Jesus. But from the very beginning he gathered twelve men to be his community, and he traveled at their pace rather than his own. Something more important than his own independence was at stake.

Such love is difficult love. It doesn't just happen. It is built, one painful step at a time, just as my love was built by choosing to apologize to the man who corralled me at the spiritual retreat. Such love may even start as charity, because we don't know how else to start. But God honors our efforts and helps us to build a greater, more two-dimensional love.

For example, when I had been in graduate school nearly a year, I had a rude awakening. I was forced to admit that I wasn't doing anything for anybody but myself. I studied, but that was so I could get the grades I wanted. I went out with friends, but that was so I would feel happy. I taught several courses, but even that was for the experience and the pay. I never did anything purely aimed at helping someone else.

Changing my pattern of behavior took a conscious effort of the will. After a dozen calls to volunteer agencies around the city, I ended up at the county court one day, role-playing with a guidance counselor what might happen if I became "big brother" for a juvenile boy in his program. Before I could back out, I was at the doorstep of a twelve-year-old who had been to court for supposed vandalism.

I remember waiting nervously on those steps, wondering if perhaps this boy would come out with a spray can and paint "GO HOME" on my sweatshirt. He didn't. And though we couldn't understand each other sometimes, Tony and I grew to enjoy each other greatly. Two years later, when I moved to Chicago, neither one of us wanted to say goodby. In fact, we didn't. We still see each other when we can.

Did I learn to love Tony as myself? Not fully. But certainly more than at first. I would have laughed if you had asked me on that first day if I loved him. How could I? I was just doing what seemed right. But now I wouldn't laugh. When I acted in faith, God blessed. God taught me *how* to love. And Tony was not the only one to receive from the experience. God loved *me* through Tony. And God taught me about myself.

That one relationship, with its odd beginning, prepared the way for me to help build other relationships, even whole communities. And I will always be grateful to Tony for his friendship.

Four

Escape
from Myself

THEORETICALLY, OF COURSE, NO PEOPLE WOULD BE BETTER suited to build community than Americans. After all, the Declaration of Independence states "that all men are created equal; that they are endowed by their Creator with certain inalienable rights."[1] This statement lays the necessary groundwork for Americans to love their neighbors "as themselves."

The problem is that independence opens the door for self-centered behavior. Instead of defending the rights of a neighbor, I am tempted to defend my own rights and let others, with their equal rights, take care of themselves. "God helps them that help themselves," as Benjamin Franklin put it.[2] So much for community.

The authors of *Habits of the Heart* argue that individualism can create the illusion that community is simply not necessary. They quote social commentator Alexis de Tocqueville, who observed Americans becoming caught up in this illusion as early as the 1830s: "Such folk owe no man anything and hardly expect anything from anybody. They form the habit of thinking of themselves in isolation and imagine that their whole destiny is in their hands."[3]

This is hard ground to walk on. I actually like the individualism of Americans. They get a lot done because they believe in what they personally can do. And they don't burden others with their needs. As a result, the history of the world is rich with the stories of Americans who stayed true to their goals, unencumbered by others: pioneers, discoverers, scientists, gunslingers, artists. Many have become legendary, like Daniel Boone, that intrepid explorer who always moved on, insisting that he needed "elbow room."

Such were my childhood heroes. As a second-grader at boarding school in Ethiopia, I began my lifelong love of reading by consuming a whole series of hardback biographies about these bigger-than-life individuals. The worn blue covers held magic to me—the promise of greatness. In the woods before bedtime, right at the magical hour of dusk, I roamed with a friend, living out their adventures. Though we stood on another continent, we charted the American West right along with Daniel Boone, facing all sorts of dangers. We relived it all, feeling indestructible. In the same way, I'm sure, children in other individualistic societies relive the lives of _their_ lengendary heroes.

I probably never will shake that childhood love of the great loners, people who seemed to live above and beyond the community, entirely self-sufficient. There is beautiful strength and vitality in people who take destiny in their own hands. Something echoes inside of me even when I hear a popular song about one of them, as when the defiant Bruce Springsteen belts out his ballad of rugged independence:

Baby, this town rips the bones from your back

It's a death trap, it's a suicide rap

We gotta get out while we're young

'Cause tramps like us, baby we were born to run . . .[4]

Like Springsteen, I'm suspicious of "the town"—the community. I don't want to get lost in it. And sometimes, if I'm honest, I'd rather believe in my own ability to transcend the community than give in to it, which seems like a compromise. In my bolder moments I may even dream that I can be bigger than anyone, if only I separate myself from the ordinary, staying out in front of the pack. And so I sing along with the "Boss":

> The highway's jammed with broken heroes
> On a last chance power drive
> Everybody's out on the run tonight
> But there's no place left to hide ...
> Baby we were born to run.[5]

I sing along. And only when I stop to think about the words—to really think—do I realize just how destructive this vision is. *Live and let die* is not the motto to choose if you truly want to live.

Who Holds Us Accountable?

One night, years ago, I got a call from the wife of a friend, who began to cry. I was surprised. She had never called me, and I'd never seen her upset.

"What's wrong?" I asked.

"Jerry's left me," she blurted out.

"Are you sure? How long has he been gone?"

"Two weeks."

I could not believe it. For two weeks she had told no one, living alone with their three-year-old son, depressed, desperate, helpless. Why?

As I look back, it becomes clear. When they came to that city (so that her husband could get into the graduate program he wanted), they left their home of many years, along with the support of his parents. They left a strong church, too, and were unable to settle on a new church. They knew no one—except me and a handful of other old friends. And in that isolation, without any community to help point the way, they lost their bearings.

Her husband was a moody, struggling artist. He decided he couldn't handle a family *and* personal goals. His family stood in the way of his goals. So he walked out. In his case, unlike Springsteen, he didn't want to take anyone with him. But that is what happens eventually if you are convinced that you have to keep breaking away. No community, not even a marriage, can last.

To this day I feel partially responsible. Their divorce was due, to some extent, to the failure of the Christian community, myself included. People under such stress need outside help. They need someone to put things back in perspective, to remind them of the strengths in their partner or weaknesses they are ignoring in themselves. They need someone to remind them of their commitment to each other. To help them stay accountable. Aren't we all tempted when we are alone to do things we would never do in the presence of others? Likewise, aren't we more honest and good when we know we are not alone?

Nigerians from Lagos are learning this the hard way. Lagos, the biggest city in the country, has a reputation for being one of the most dangerous in Africa. People are constantly being robbed. In one case a man saw thieves taking his car. He chased them in another car until he caught up with them—and then, to his amazement, he was arrested because the thieves convinced the police that they were the real owners.

When I asked a Nigerian friend how such things could happen, he said, "It's because people don't know each other anymore. In the village these things don't happen. But as soon as people go to the city, they think they can do anything and no one will know."

He sighed, almost embarrassed to talk about it, and I could tell that he longed for the old values that he had grown up with, outside the city. He felt helpless, watching urbanization dissolve all the old codes of behavior, taking with them the accountability that had once existed.

A Longing for Neighbors

By contrast, in the West (or what might better be called the North) we've already gone through urbanization. And supposedly we have adjusted. But I think we too, secretly, long for the old community values.

Why, for example, did Garrison Keillor captivate so many with his radio program "A Prairie Home Companion," based on his childhood in a small town in Minnesota? He struck a chord that resonated in the heart of America. Was it simply nostalgia? I don't think so. Keillor gave form to a deep longing for community—a desire for a good place where people know each other fully, a place *where we all help each other to stay good.*

Consider one of his more popular broadcasts, when Keillor read a letter from a fictional friend who had just turned forty. Worn down by the cares of being a husband and father, and dissatisfied with his job, this friend wrote that he had stepped out on his porch to wait for a ride to Chicago, where he would attend a conference. He would travel with his coworker, a beautiful and lonely woman who had brought new life into his dull routine. As he explained to Keillor, his coworker had become an encouragement to him because she laughed at his jokes, commented on his wit, trusted in him. And so, as he waited for her that night, he realized he was thinking of adultery.

Disturbed, he looked around at the houses that he had known for so many years, and he contemplated his neighbors. "They lived a life that, to me, seemed decent, and loving, and honorable."

Suddenly it struck him: "I saw that although I thought my sins could be secret, that they would be no more secret than an earthquake." As he imagined, his infidelity would literally shake the houses around him: noxious fumes would spill out of the grade-school water heaters, a teacher would grow weary and jettison South America from her geography notes, the supermarket owner would disregard the expiration date on his sausages and leave them displayed. In other words, if he gave in to his desire to do as he pleased, then eventually others would follow his example and betray the community too.[6]

At that point the power of good that existed in that little neighborhood in Lake Wobegon became so strong that it brought the man back from the brink, saving him from disaster. He didn't commit adultery. He didn't follow the urges of Springsteen's hero, who was born to run. In this way, community rescued him.

In the same way, community can rescue each of us. It can rescue us from ourselves. Even better, community can help us to *become* ourselves—to become who we are really meant to be.

After finishing his fictional letter, Keillor didn't go into how adultery would have affected his friend personally. But it probably would have damaged more than the neighborhood. It probably would have ruined the man himself.

Paradoxically, when we break away from the community, demanding to find out who we are on our own, we lose ourselves instead. It's our friends and family—even our enemies—who know us best. We can see only our front side. They see us from all sides, even the back. And we see ourselves fully only in relationship to them. We need the community as much as it needs us.

The Discipline of Community

I know this is not a new theme for people who live in democratic and individualistic societies. Maybe the problem is not recognizing the need for community; it is acting. If our society has been shouting at us our whole lives: "Be your own person; live for yourself," then how likely are we to want a community? It's like asking cats, independent as they are, to hit the streets, doglike, in packs.

So we have to be intentional about community, or it won't happen. If we can't get it any other way, we need to build it. To start with, maybe even our friendships have to be intentional.

One of my closest friends became close to me because we agreed to meet every week for a year. We didn't let anything get in the way, and by the end of the year we didn't *want* anything to get in the way. We had become brothers. We were willing to share anything. In fact, one week we found ourselves discussing a novel by Charles Williams which portrayed characters living out substitutionary love, and suddenly we made a pact to try it. Each week we shared what burdened us, then let it go for the other person (with God's help) to carry. As the days went by, I prayed regularly that the Lord would release Drew from the weight of his worries, his fears, his temptations. Mentally, I shouldered that weight for myself. He did the same for me. And it was amazing how supported we felt. Each of us knew he was not alone.

One such friendship can multiply into more. Be intentional about forming a whole group of friends. What's important is not so much what the group does as that it *is* a group.

For example, several young Christian couples in Saskatchewan began to meet monthly simply to share their interest in literature. Each month they talked about a book they had agreed to read. They grappled with the issues raised by Christian writers and non-Christian ones. Then they began to try other things—discussing videos, studying portions of the Bible, just praying. Others joined them until there were ten or twelve people in all. I spent only one evening with this group, years ago, but I will not forget it because I felt strangely rejuvenated. Nothing remarkable happened. We grilled hamburgers outside on the lawn, then watched the film *Witness* and talked about it. These were things I could have done anywhere. But I left strengthened—and that was because the people were so obviously at ease with each other and so obviously seeking the same depth of relationship. They were *people who could count on each other.*

The Body of Christ in a Barn
In the end, the size and strength of a community depends on the willingness of its members to give themselves to living in relationship. You can't stay part of a community and still make all your decisions based purely on personal goals. Some evening you will find you can't meet because there is too much work to do, or the ball game is on the same night, or you just don't feel like it. And next thing, you will find yourself in another city pursuing a job with a higher salary.

If we aim to reach only personal goals, eventually we will find ourselves alienated. But if we aim to reach people, we will have a community. We may even surprise ourselves by forming a community which is larger than we had thought possible.

For nearly ten years now my parents have been part of a Christian community in Kansas that formed simply because people weren't finding community in their churches. They came from a cross-section of churches—Baptist, Mennonite, Lutheran and a variety of independent churches—but they all complained that the churches didn't satisfy their need for fellowship. At church, people came and went, exchanging a few words. They focused for an hour on worshipping together, then broke away to their separate lives, not to see each other until the next Sunday.

The people in the Wellspring group continued to attend their old churches. But during the week they came together on a farm. As one member put it, he loved to be with them because it was the only organization he knew that came together mainly just to be together.

Rather than hampering them, that relaxed attitude has actually freed the Wellspring folks to accomplish much, and it has kept their work in perspective. With a lot of volunteer effort, they have converted an old barn into a rustic meeting hall. They've turned a corn crib into a bunkhouse. And another shed has become a shower stall. With these humble facilities, the farm has become a conference center, where people from Kansas and beyond come together for regular meetings and conferences. They meet to discuss family life, to explore their spirituality, to host international students during holidays, to worship, to study theology or philosophy or literature, to simply play.

The group itself plans the conferences, taking on the roles of a staff: greeter, cook, emcee, speaker, child-care supervisor, entertainment coordinator, musician and so on. By working together, exploring different roles, they discover themselves in ways they never could alone. The community affirms the gifts they have and encourages them to develop, and so they have a sense of belonging.

I say all this from firsthand experience. Even though Cathy and I live in Chicago now, we still feel a part of that community, and we return whenever we can. Why? Because there we experience being affirmed for who we are as unique members of the body of Christ.

More Than a Morning Service

When my parents decided, five years ago, to move onto the farm where Wellspring meets, joining the two other families who were there, they built a log cabin as their house. They shipped in logs from two Wisconsin cabins which German settlers had built in the 1800s. The family congregated to do the building, and we invited anyone to join us if they wanted to be part of the project. Each day someone new showed up, sometimes whole families at a time, who wanted to lift logs into position, drill holes for the wooden pegs that held them tight, nail down shingles, put up dry wall, hang curtains, wallpaper. We were the closest thing to an Amish barnraising that you could get in Kansas.

On the morning when we began the chinking (putting cement between the logs), so many people showed up—over twenty in the end—that we were able to complete the outside layer by sunset! The sense of community that day was wonderful. Everyone had a part to play, from the older women (who served food) to the children (who carried cement to the workers on pieces of plywood).

When the house was finally done, we had a calligrapher—also from Wellspring—create an eight-foot rough wooden plaque with these words burned onto it: "The builder of a house has greater honor than the house itself" (Heb 3:3). Everyone who had helped was asked to sign it; over eighty signatures were collected, many in different languages. Now, when I sit in the living room of that house, reading those names, I feel fortunate to have been part of such an experience—not just the building, but the cooperation that went into the building.

It seems to me that the church, our ultimate community, should be a place where people live together and build together, not just a place to sing hymns while privately waiting to get home. By participating in each other's lives, rather than protecting our own, we are finally able to become who we are. In community we are liberated from our loneliness, set free to become whole people.

Five

Released
to Risk

EVERY YEAR—OR EVERY FEW MONTHS IF I'M FORTUNATE —I have a moment when I feel the fullness of life. One of those moments came during a trip to England. Not surprisingly, it was during a concert. Music unlocks a door in me—lets the world get in, lets me get out.

Ken Medema was the performer, singing solo while standing at a keyboard. A single electronic keyboard is not much to work with, especially if you are blind, and Medema *is* blind. Yet he performed with incredible boldness, jabbing the notes out of his keyboard, shouting with uninhibited gusto. He held nothing back.

Halfway through the concert Medema suddenly launched into a song about the existential joy of being young, and something happened inside me. He was celebrating youth while mourning the loss of it, belting out a series of powerful lyrics. While he played, he danced at the keyboard, swinging one arm. He became a boy again, grayhaired, blind, but refusing to be old. He became a child leaping for the sheer pleasure of leaping. He sang about climbing mountains in the moonlight, swimming rivers in the rain, leaping to the stars, diving into the ocean to sing with whales.

I watched and thought to myself, *Here's someone who looks hand-icapped but isn't. I want to be just as alive as he is, but instead I often feel handicapped, struggling just to stay awake. Why?*

I stared at Medema, then down at the shadows from my drinking glass. The shadows seemed to dance on the tablecloth. A white paper doily seemed to dance too, lifted by some mysterious breeze. As he shouted out in ecstasy, in longing, in mortal grief, I could not stop the swelling inside of me, until it burst up my throat and squeezed out of my eyes. Something huge was released, let go.

Rocked Awake

I'm not satisfied with the quality of my life. Yes, I'm comfortable—better off than the vast majority of human beings. But I'm not sat-isfied. Whole days go by, sometimes weeks, and they feel lost. It maddens me. I've been given so many years, maybe seventy-five, eighty-five if I'm fortunate, but so much of that time seems to go by in a fog. When I am done, I fear I will look back and find I lived only twenty years altogether. That the rest was just putting in time, like a hostage chained and blindfolded, waiting.

Even though Medema brought all this to the surface for me, up to that point I had been uncomfortable with his performances as the conference musician. Here we were in Sheffield, England, six hundred delegates gathered from around the world to talk about Christian communications. There were people from the Philippines and Nigeria and Bolivia, from Egypt and Romania. But we were listening to noth-ing but loud American music!

I couldn't imagine my Asian and African associates shouting and dancing the way Medema did. It was so loud, so defiant—a direct contrast to the gentleness of Solon, a Nepali friend, or to the dignity of Lukio from Kenya. It didn't seem to fit. But as I listened on that last night, I put aside my attempt to be crossculturally sensitive and let myself be purely Western. No wonder we shout when we sing: we are trying to hear ourselves and to make others hear. Americans particularly (the middle-class at least) are so soundproofed and padded by wide lawns and hermetically sealed houses that we have to make extra efforts to stay awake and aware. We have to scream, kicking and punching and tearing at the surface of our existence. Through rock music we break free, even if for only a fleeting moment, from all the convenience and comfort that surround our day-to-day life, lulling us into spiritual sleep.

For Christians in a convenience culture, it can be so hard to stay *spiritually* awake. I remember, for example, one vacation during my skeptical college years when several cousins visited at our family home in Riley, Kansas. My brothers and I talked with them late into the night, as only cousins can do—sprawled out across the sofa and living room carpet, telling stories, laughing, being philosophical. Somehow we got onto religion, a subject that had seemed taboo because of apparent differences between our parents' worldviews.

In a moment of complete candor, one of them said, "You know, I'm becoming more interested in religion, but I don't know how to think about spiritual things. I never learned to think spiritually."

Even that night, as we reclined there, well-fed, warm, secure, I had to fight the feeling that this was just an academic exercise, something interesting but not vital. My cousin, who felt the yawning vacuum building inside her, knew better. Yet I could see she too had trouble comprehending why the spirit was important. Psyche maybe. But spirit? What was that?

It surprised her. And why not? At the time, she was launching on a career in medicine, a career based on physical laws. What did the world of the spirit matter to her, a person sure to live comfortably, and to do it by making others more comfortable?

The British rock group Pink Floyd has it right: in the West we are "comfortably numb."[1] Though my cousin didn't need it, rock is a wake-up call. For a moment, all the pent-up energy surges to the surface. The soul surfaces too. What it breathes is not always pure, or good, particularly when it comes from performers with no moral framework. But still it is better than nothing.

In the U.S., then, it's no surprise that a whole culture has developed around rock. It began when the hippies, disillusioned with prosperity, broke loose. Like other religious seekers, some of them made vows of poverty. They wandered without possessions. They dressed down. That was their way of becoming spiritually attuned. And even though many of them fell back to sleep spiritually, due to drugs or sexual addictions, they at least recognized the prison of comfort and named it out loud. With the help of rock, they experienced moments of alertness, defying the ease of their culture.

You don't have to be a "fat cat" to fall asleep, though. The human condition is to doze. Aleksandr Solzhenitsyn would understand. By contrast, he woke up spiritually in much more difficult circumstances—after years of bitter forced labor in the prison camps of Siberia. There he secretly hid notes to himself and memorized the events that eventually became his gigantic work *Gulag Archipelago,* a printed memorial to all those who suffered and died—unknown, uncared for—in the Gulag. But, ironically, Solzhenitsyn's personal reaction to labor camp was to bless it, because it was there that he discovered that "the meaning of earthly existence lies not, as we have grown used to thinking, in prospering, but . . . in the development of the soul."[2]

Communist Siberia and middle-class America? They are worlds apart. Yet in both places—in all places really—meaning lies not in prospering but in the development of the soul. And finding that meaning is always a struggle. It's just that the struggle is intensified for those of us who are part of the dominant middle class in affluent societies, precisely because we are so able to prosper. It keeps us from nurturing our souls. We're too comfortable to be spiritual. We think we have it so easy. Safe. Secure. We think we will be able to pursue God better without danger or hardship. And yet it works in just the opposite way. Nothing is more difficult than to grow spiritually when comfortable.

With security surrounding us, we may need a radical change to bring us to our senses. In my case, for six months I was privileged to live with the poor in the Philippines, learning from them. As part of an internship in development work, I moved in with a family of squatters at the heart of the great, sprawling city of Manila, squeezed in with the fifteen million other souls who called it home. Difficult as that experience was, it did more to restore my spirit than any number of theoretical discussions.

Life in a Slum

I lived in a little plywood shack on stilts. If you followed the ditch that ran under the house, full of bottle caps and human waste, it led to a filthy river called, paradoxically, the San Juan. The squatters lived there only because no one else wanted to be so close to so much toxic waste, particularly since the San Juan flooded almost every year.

The Gasces family gave me a fourth of their one-room home, keeping the rest for themselves and their two little boys, Tom and Jojit. We built two plywood walls and a narrow door so I could have privacy; when I lay down on my cot, I could touch all four walls at once. But even this tight little room was a luxury most squatters did not have—a space of my own.

Young skeptic that I was, I didn't trust their religion any more than mine. They had a corner where they kept the required paraphernalia: a calendar with a picture of Jesus pointing to his sacred heart, bright red and surrounded by rays of gold; and a plaster Mary, white as pure snow and draped gently with light blue robes.

As far as I could tell, they never prayed before this corner, but they put strings of sampaguita flowers around Mary's neck, and they wouldn't get rid of her for anything. Everyone had such icons; to live without them was foolhardy. Evil spirits had immediate access in those homes.

I sometimes wanted to laugh at their fears, such as on Good Friday when they tried to stop me from leaving the house because it would assuredly result in an accident. "Superstition" I had learned to call it back home in the U.S., where religion was more sophisticated, more rational—and *less* spiritual. What I couldn't see at first was that their fear was merely the other side of their amazing capacity to believe. They truly believed in God, in Satan, in the spirits that did war. These were not just mental constructs.

While there, I attended a little church that had been started by a tough young minister. Jun Paragas had moved into the area with his wife and baby to minister to the squatters. In fact, it was through him that I had found my home with the Gasces.

One Sunday, Jun, in his usual forthright way, led a service to destroy what he called family idols. His congregation didn't do this indoors, quietly. They did it outside to make it a testimony to the community. Members of the church who wanted to be freed from their dependence on icons carried the icons out to a small, smoldering dump, where they proceeded to smash and burn them.

It was a bright, hot day, and I felt very odd standing there with our formal little group in the midst of all the mango scraps and broken glass. It was hard to imagine evil spirits while standing in such glaring sunlight. I remember in particular Aling Nena, a former alcoholic who had converted to the faith and found miraculous healing from her addiction. Aling Nena had a terrible time releasing her Virgin Mary. She stifled a small scream and danced forward, pleading. Jun paused with his hammer aloft, put it down and walked over to console her. They prayed—we all prayed for her to be freed of the fears that bound her. She nodded slightly, confident of what she wanted, and the hammer dropped onto the plaster, breaking it open in a white burst. Immediately, she thanked God for new freedom, a freedom she said she already felt.

How strange it all was to me! Why? Because it was a spiritual happening, not physical. Something occurred there that was as real as the broken plaster, but invisible. A whole dialogue went on like the half-understood Tagalog conversations all around me, only more for-

eign, more difficult for me, the young Western materialist, to comprehend.

We may need to become iconoclastic if we are to be set free spiritually. Aling Nena was afraid that she wouldn't be protected or safe
without her Virgin Mary. Those of us from the First World are afraid
that we won't be safe without other icons: a salary to cover all needs,
insurance for every imaginable problem, credit cards to cover unexpected costs, a home in a safe neighborhood, enough cars to avoid
inconvenience, all the comforts that money can provide.

We pay heavily for such security, and not just in money. For "what
good will it be for a man if he gains the whole world, yet forfeits his
soul?" (Mt 16:26).

Out of the Cocoon

Christ once said, "It is easier for a camel to go through the eye of a
needle than for a rich man to enter the kingdom of God" (Mt 19:24).
He knew that living inside the cocoon of prosperity, people are cut off
from reality. Outside it, they are able to see and feel again. Their
spirits awaken.

How then to get out?

A good starting place is to let go of the things we don't need. It is
truly amazing to me how little I really do need, if only I am willing
to experiment with giving it up. Otherwise, it all becomes padding.
And enough padding becomes a prison.

The dangers of ownership are depicted wonderfully in a film from
the early eighties—*My Dinner with Andre*. Wally, a homebody play-
wright, has reluctantly agreed to eat with Andre, a theater director
who used to be a friend before he apparently lost his wits. Over
dinner, the eccentric Andre captivates Wally with a long story. He
tells how he roamed the world, searching for reality. Back now, he
thinks most people spend the bulk of their life in a sort of dream
world.

Wally, who rather likes living a protected, insular life, struggles to

get a grip on what Andre is saying, and the only handle he comes up
with is his electric blanket, which was given to him and his wife as
a Christmas present. The conversation that follows goes to the very
heart of the matter:

Andre: Well, I wouldn't put an electric blanket on for anything . . .
First, I'd be worried that I might get electrocuted. I don't trust
technology. But I mean, the main thing, Wally, is that that kind
of comfort just separates you from reality in a very direct way.

Wally: You mean—

Andre: I mean, if you *don't* have that electric blanket and your
apartment is cold—and you need to put on another blanket, or go
into the closet and pile up coats on top of the blankets you have,
well, then, you *know* it's cold. . . . And that sets up a link of things.
You have compassion for the person—is the person *next* to you
cold? Are there other people in the world who are cold? What a cold
night! I *like* the cold. My God, I don't really want a blanket—I
never realized—it's *fun* being cold! I can snuggle up against you
even more because it's cold—all sorts of things occur to you. But,
turn on that electric blanket, and it's like taking a tranquilizer, or
it's like being lobotomized by watching television. I think you enter
the dream world again. I mean, what does it do to us, Wally, to live
in an environment where something as massive as the seasons and
the cold and the winter don't in any way affect us? . . .

Wally: Yes, but I mean, I would *never* give up my electric blanket,
Andre, because New York is cold, our apartment is cold in the
winter. It's a difficult environment. Our lives are tough enough as
it is. I mean, I'm not trying to get rid of the few things that provide
relief and comfort. On the contrary, I'm looking for *more* comfort,
because the world is very abrasive . . .

Andre: But, Wally, don't you see that comfort can be dangerous?
I mean, you like to be comfortable, and I like to be comfortable, too,
but don't you see that comfort can lull you into a dangerous tran-
quillity?[3]

We all need to own certain things to achieve a degree of comfort. Wally sees that. But what Andre is arguing for is a limit. He has learned that "owning comfort" can become a need so strong that it enslaves him. That obsession is what Andre, in spite of his extremist views, has broken free of.

Do we really need the electric blanket? The extra shoes? The new drapes? All those books?

Too Safe for Our Own Good
Letting go of possessions breaks the bonds of comfort. But if I want to be freed all the way, in the biblical sense, if I want to go beyond giving up what isn't needed, the next step is for me to prayerfully listen to my conscience, then to take risks. Not just any risks, but the risks that God demands.

Sometimes we are too safe to be alive. Stripping oneself of wealth takes away the numbness only for a while, if the soul is not transformed. For wealth itself is not the problem. It's my attitude—an attitude of fear that makes me protect myself excessively, that demands comfort. It's that attitude that determines whether or not I stay trapped inside the cocoon, trapped in soft and sleepy blindness. And when that defensive attitude stands in the way, there's no remedy better than simply *doing the difficult thing.*

It may be as small as stopping to help a stranger stranded on the highway. It may be driving into the city one night a week and parking in a rough neighborhood so I can serve at a soup kitchen. It may be even larger—taking in a rent-free boarder who needs a safe home, changing my job, adopting a child. These risks, made with such effort, will wrench me back into reality. They are like fresh air introduced into a garage full of carbon monoxide.

Without listening to God, I do not know what is truly healthy for myself. Risking for risk's sake is not the answer. But risking for God's sake is. And God is always wanting us to risk for his sake, just as his Son Jesus did. Thankfully, he knows that taking such risks is difficult, and he will not ask more than we can give.

On a flight out of Ethiopia several years ago, I met a gentle, kind-spirited man who took unusual interest in my wife and me. He seemed delighted to meet us and he was curious to know our stories, as well as to share his own. He turned out to be the chairman for the board of a major relief-and-development organization.

Hamilton was there with a film crew, making a documentary on hunger in East Africa. In fact, as I learned from a crew member, he had paid for most of the filming out of his own pocket. During our conversation, he admitted reluctantly that he was an attorney by trade. For years he had made his living (and apparently a very good one at that) by doing legal work, but he had never found satisfaction in it. Then he became involved with relief-and-development work.

"For the first time, I felt as if my life had meaning," he said, laughing sheepishly. "I mean that. As an attorney, you've got to wonder sometimes if you have any meaning at all."

In my opinion, Hamilton showed that he had broken out of the shell of comfort. No person enslaved to security would have risked going into Ethiopia at that time—when Eritrean rebels had pushed within eighty miles of Addis Ababa and when Colonel Mengistu was rumored to be on the verge of toppling from power. Nor would he have traveled into the destitute areas where this film crew had to work, risking the diseases that rage through. But Hamilton had, and as a result he was spiritually alive. He had been set free from the illusion that his comfort, like Aling Nena's Virgin Mary, would somehow magically make life livable, worthwhile. To him, it was a delight that people around the world were coming to Christ, because they saw Christians like himself giving of their wealth and risking involvement, no matter how stressful or dangerous that might be.

Hamilton was unusual. He had the strength to become spiritually alive while staying wealthy. Most do not have that strength. Saint Francis, for one, knew that he needed to break from wealth altogether. He literally stripped the clothes off his body so that they would not stand between him and God. He did not want any comfort if it meant captivity.

But Francis was rewarded for his action with riches beyond compare, for in taking that step he learned the truth stated so well by Thomas à Kempis, a monk who lived only one hundred years later, in the fourteenth century: "O my soul, thou can'st not be fully comforted, nor have perfect refreshment, except in God, the Comforter of the poor, and Patron of the humble."[4]

Each of us needs to be set free from comfort. We need to ask, *How much do I really need?* Any more can become a trap. And to prove our willingness to live with less, we need to take the risks that God asks of us. There is wonderful liberation in letting go.

Six

Truth
Set Loose

ONE EVENING WHILE LEADING A WORKSHOP FOR EDITORS in Kampala, Uganda, I ate with two Ugandans who had recently gotten master's degrees in the United States. To get to the restaurant, we drove down a dozen dark streets, past the gaping doors of ramshackle canteens, each lit from inside by a bare bulb and emblazoned with the universal red-and-white Coke sign. The restaurant boasted fried chicken and the jukebox threw out American tunes, which followed us as we drifted through a curtain of beaded strings to a table in the far corner.

Thankfully, the food came quickly—it was 9:00 p.m. When it arrived, I ate with gusto, dipping the chicken in watery ketchup (provided apparently as a part of the authentic American dining). As I ate, I listened to my companions voice their frustrations. While studying in the U.S. at a Protestant college, they had become accustomed to a more flexible way of life. Now everything seemed insufferably slow and difficult, and the people seemed narrow-minded. My friends wanted to try new things, different things, but it was taking too long.

They were thankful, though, because they *had* returned, and had come back with their faith intact. They described friends who never came back—who were so spiritually disoriented they never recovered.

One of those lost ones had gone with them to the same Christian college, but as an undergraduate. After a year he had given up on his studies. He wandered around in a daze. When they asked him what was wrong, he replied, "I came here too soon. I didn't know who I was or what I believed. Now I'll never know."

"What did he mean?" I asked.

"In the U.S.," they explained, "nothing is clear. It all 'depends.' People are too relativistic."

One of them had taken a course in ethics while in the U.S. He was dismayed at how little consensus there was, even among Christians, on what was truly right or wrong. In one situation an action might be wrong, in another right. And the American students had reached a place where they would allow for almost any behavior, depending on the person's circumstances or background.

As these two described the moral paralysis they had felt in that Christian college, I realized how deeply rooted relativism is, not only in secular society but among Christians as well. Because those living in modern democratic societies insist on living so separately, our concepts of good and evil are not verified or challenged by others. They become reduced to personal preferences. We are unable or unwilling to see truth as something that can be confirmed by the community. I'm okay and you're okay, just as long as we both keep our beliefs to ourselves.

Road to Nowhere

Answering such relativism is virtually impossible. That's why it is so debilitating.

I remember I once took a Greyhound bus from Kansas City to Chicago and ended up in one of those conversations that occur on buses. Perhaps you've experienced them. Generally, they skip from "Hello" to "What's your theory of the universe?"

That day, I sat next to a weatherbeaten, whiskery man in his seventies, the sort who didn't look likely to talk. That should have been my first clue that he was, in fact, a Greyhound philosopher. I had hardly settled into my seat when he went to work, testing my "theory." He got me to admit I was a Christian, then to admit I believed Jesus when he said "I am the Way, the Truth, and the Life." At that point, he pounced.

"The way I see it," he said, "there's a lot of people traveling to Chicago today. Some are flying and some are driving or taking the train. And you and me just happen to be on a bus. But we're *all* going there, so what does it matter *how* we go? That's the way I see it."

What could I say? For such a person, coming to an agreement is impossible. That's because agreement doesn't even matter. Every point of view is valid.

Today, I still don't know how to answer such an argument. Except perhaps in this way: "What about all the people who aren't convinced they should go to Chicago? The ones who are driving to Los Angeles or New York, or the ones who plan to get off the bus before Chicago, in the town called Normal, Illinois? If Chicago really is the best destination, what about all the travelers who are headed the wrong direction?"

The problem with wholesale relativism is that it becomes absurd at some point. Is being an alcoholic really a viable alternative lifestyle, one that we should respect? Is excessive buying? Is Satanism?

At some point we have to draw the line. And I say *we* intentionally, because *we* are less likely to be wrong about defining the limits than *I;* that is, as long as one person does not dominate or manipulate the opinions of the rest.

If we do not intentionally work toward such agreement, each of us will eventually demand more than having a vote: we will demand our own way. The result is a people at odds with themselves, with no common commitment, no direction. Lost relativists. To borrow an expression from the rock group Talking Heads, such people are "on the road to nowhere."[1]

Personal Opinion Plays God

Of course, relativism isn't exclusively American. It is evident everywhere today, as an unavoidable byproduct of modernity, and it is perhaps stronger among Europeans than Americans.

One of the strongest statements of relativism I've heard came from a German, a friend who was an atheist. Having admitted to her that I sometimes struggled with doubt, not being able to see God or experience him tangibly, I told her that, nevertheless, I was convinced that God exists and that he is a personal Creator, not some sort of abstract life force or figment of my imagination.

"That seems so clear to me," I explained, "because it's impossible for me to think that all the complex order of the universe—the planets spinning on their scheduled courses, the grass shooting out of the ground each spring, the two of us understanding this complex code called language—that all these things just *happen*. Nothing that beautiful and organized just happens."

She replied, "You may be right, but don't try to convince other people. They should believe what they want!"

I didn't try to convince *her*. After all, no one is convinced who is not willing to be convinced. But internally I groaned. *How far would she go in enshrining personal opinion? To the point of applauding anyone who has an idea, no matter how dangerous or destructive it might be? Would she applaud a Nazi?* I knew she wouldn't. She was too good a person for that. Too honest.

The Reign of Relativism

Respecting one another's views is one thing, but treating them as sacred and untouchable is another. That leads to all sorts of delusions. Nonetheless, the nonsensical "philosophy" of relativism is prevalent everywhere. And nowhere is it stronger than in the university, where it has stormed and overthrown the very seat of knowledge. There it reigns supreme, spreading its doctrine by royal decree, unchallenged, preeminent, all-wise.

In his bestseller *The Closing of the American Mind*, the late Allan Bloom argues convincingly that relativism is unraveling the fabric of U.S. society. He laments that college students come to the university already infected with it, ready to accept any and every opinion because they have been taught that tolerance is the highest of all virtues. For them, the only enemy is "the man who is not open to everything."[2]

Bloom is right, I fear, in this description. The university is merely reaping what it has sown. Students come to the university with their minds closed because the university has already shut their parents' minds and their teachers' minds, even their ministers' minds. The university has so successfully propagated relativism that now it doesn't need to. Still, it goes on doing it, as any institution does with safe, status-quo concepts. Although Bloom may not have been teaching relativism, for every professor who isn't, ten are.

Why am I so outraged by the dominating influence of relativism in the university? I ask myself.

Because I have watched friends fall victim to it. I have watched them become enamored with the wisdom of professors who profess nothing, who believe that every position is arguable. Then I have watched them get snarled in a swirling chaos of ideas. And finally I have seen them sucked dry of every last bit of trust and confidence that they once had, becoming lost people, unable to commit themselves to anything because commitment is impossible in a world where all positions are equally valid.

Some of them, in their cynicism, reach a point where no position can be trusted anymore. I think of one friend, in particular, who came from England as a fellow graduate student in English literature—a brilliant student who returned to finish a Ph.D. at Oxford. He loved literary criticism, especially the theory of deconstruction.

My friend hosted me at Oxford several years after we had finished our master's degrees. As we walked through the lush green park surrounding Magdalen College—that school where the clear-minded

C. S. Lewis taught—he told me that he couldn't maintain his Christian faith any longer.

"Why?" I asked.

"Because I don't have any language for faith. I can't talk that way. I can't even think in those categories."

Deconstructive theory, a byproduct of popular relativism, had robbed him of the ability to "know"—which is, in reality, to *believe.* There he was, studying at one of the greatest centers of human knowledge, and knowing wasn't even possible. The only absolute left was that absolutes were impossible.

In brief, the deconstructionist says, "All right, you naive person, you don't really believe what you are saying. I can prove it. I'll show you all the places where you contradict yourself. If you were honest with me, you would have to admit that, really, you doubt your own premises. So much for so-called 'Truth.' "

A valid claim! Any person trying to deliver a point of view *does* come to the moment of presentation with doubts. And for the sake of proving a point, that person is likely to override doubts, leaving subtle contradictions like clues that lead back to the original doubts. I should know. Even as I am writing this, I have to admit that I have doubts about my own argument.

But what many deconstructionists overlook, if I am allowed to use their own tactics, is that they themselves believe in Truth! For all their talk about contradictions, they are confidently committed to the truth that there is no secure Truth. And they marshal all their innate logic to prove that point. In fact, while making their claim to this truth, they rely on the very language they distrust in others.

If, indeed, everything one says is a contradiction, then why say anything? Nothing is trustworthy. But in reality, we all secretly *do* agree on much. We trust that a shared meaning is possible in certain words and actions, and we trust most of what we hear or see—not all of it, but much. There's a lot that we *do* agree on, and the deconstructionists often simply refuse to acknowledge those agreements.

Agreeing to Disagree?

I think I know how my friend got to where he ended up mentally. I don't dare say that I know the whole truth and nothing but the truth, but I *think* that he took all that deconstructive theory to its logical end. If each of us has separate, insupportable worlds of meaning, then there is nothing that is universally true. And Christianity, which is based on the premise of certain universal truths, is nothing but a hoax.

I don't want to be simplistic in responding, because I have had some of the same doubts. The fact is that the multitudes of Christian denominations that have sprung up over the centuries, with all their divergent doctrines, are clear proof Christians don't agree on who God is or how a Christian should act. We contradict ourselves. A friend from Delhi, India, argues bitterly that the main reason the missions movement in India has had such limited success is precisely because of denominational divisiveness. The missionaries imported with them all their petty differences, seeming to present not one faith but a hundred.

Our visions are narrowed by personal biases, so that we see in a limited way, like people in tunnels. And yet, I still say that if we set aside the differences for a moment, we *do* see much that is the same, confirming it for each other. And together we get closer to the Truth than if we seek it apart, blind to our own blind spots. I say that Truth is bigger than any of us—that only God is big enough to "know" it— and that is why we need to help each other. It will take all of us, holding hands, to encircle the Truth.

Maybe I am not that far removed from the deconstructionists after all. I have a feeling that in theory they would agree with me that what we call Truth is known best in community, since they insist so adamantly on keeping the dialogue open, and since they assert that no one person has all the answers. I just wish they would admit that agreement is legitimate and that it may even confirm Truth.

People have so much in common, regardless of their cultural or philosophical backgrounds. No matter how different they are, they *can*

learn to understand each other—at least to a great extent. Even if they
start with different languages, give them time and they will have
taught each other the meanings of their words, their linguistic sym-
bols. Where there is confusion, they will work it out. If this weren't
possible, they wouldn't accomplish anything, no matter how simple.
One of them would ask for bread and the other would pass along a
handful of pebbles. One would say "I love you," and the other would
respond with a slap.

The fact is, that kind of interaction actually happens. But it gets
corrected eventually: "Why did you slap me when I said I loved you?"

"Oh, I'm sorry. I misunderstood. I thought you said I had a face like
a tuna fish."

The average person knows, through common sense, that somehow
we can get through these disagreements. Not always, but often.

The Politics of Tolerance

So why do people still tiptoe cautiously around beliefs, secretly fearing
that they will be misunderstood?

For example, countless times I have talked with others about my
faith and heard the qualifying statement: "I don't have any problem
with other religions. People have a right to believe what they want
to." Quickly they assert that they will accept any point of view—
apparently because they have already concluded agreement is impossible.

That's not the way most Christians from traditional societies would
respond. It is a characteristically "modern" habit or, to be more current, "postmodern." The dominant ethic in postmodern societies like
Europe and in nations like Canada, Australia and the U.S., has become
one of tolerance. Supposedly, a person should tolerate *anything:* the
only sin is to act intolerant. People are so affected by this ethic, in
fact, that they become afraid to say anything that might be seen as
a judgment or even as an influence on the otherwise sacred private
views of an individual.

I'm no exception to the rule. That is why the relativist in me shouts out, *Be fair! There are strengths to the relativist way of believing.* And that's true. Relativism allows us to be moderate—more open to others with different points of view. It also protects us from dangerous extremes. And that is something we should be thankful for. In less-developed nations, by contrast, there is sometimes a higher incidence of absolutism, bringing with it severe consequences. For instance, members of one Christian group in Burma are so literal in their interpretation of the Bible that they have actually cut off their hands or gouged out their eyes if they felt these caused them to sin. That hardly qualifies as healthy Christianity.

And many people from more traditional societies are thankful to immigrate to the West. One Eritrean, for example, speaks warmly of Canada, where he now lives. "People in other countries will even kill each other over religious disagreements. Not here. People in Canada are much more tolerant."

On the other hand, in those traditional societies you don't find people so afraid to claim their faith publicly. Even when they have to be careful due to overt religious persecution, they are surprisingly quick to affirm their faith. I receive letters from associates in Africa and Asia. Many of them live in societies hostile to Christianity, and yet they begin boldly, "Greetings in the name of our Lord Jesus Christ."

Similarly, at meetings in certain countries people will introduce themselves this way, "My name is Mugo, and I am saved—thanks be to God." For them, beliefs can and should be public; they are not an embarrassment.

Perhaps we could learn from each other. Traditional Christians could learn from the tolerant point of view among Christians in more modern and relativistic societies, the same point of view that made Jesus say, when asked to judge a woman caught in adultery, "If any one of you is without sin, let him be the first to throw a stone at her." And relativistic Christians could learn from the firmness of other

Christians, the same firmness that Jesus showed after the accusers had gone, when he said to the adulteress, "Go now and leave your life of sin" (Jn 8:7-11). In Jesus we see a perfect balance of openness and firmness. And we should strive toward it.

Truth Comes Out of the Closet

Much of the firmness I have seen in Christians in non-Western countries begins in churches where people are invited to share their experience of God—their testimonies, in effect. To learn how to speak my convictions to non-Christians, I find I must first of all break down the barriers of privacy that separate me from fellow *Christians*. For instance, I'm delighted that, at the church I presently attend, the head minister has introduced what he calls an "Emmanuel Moment." In each service, we pause briefly so that people can share how they have seen God at work in their lives.

If truth resides in God, then this sort of "safe" sharing is the beginning point—simply acknowledging his presence to other believers. As much as I shrink from such public commitment, there is freedom in it. If I assert myself against the unspoken demand for a private faith, I find myself becoming less daunted by the thought that others, even Christians, might not approve. I begin to be more bold in stating my faith.

My soccer coach is an atheist. I'm pretty sure of that because he taunts me for going to church when we have a Sunday game. And if I miss a shot on goal, he is likely to yell something like, "Bascom, maybe you need to pray harder."

But I think Glynn likes me, and that's because I yell back when *he* misses a shot, "Glynn, maybe I'm not the only one who needs to pray more." We spar all the time, and I have come to like him very much, despite his grievances with God. At least he cares whether God exists. We have that in common.

Nevertheless, it can be lonely being the solo Christian. So I was delighted when another player stepped into the fray during a game:

"Glynn, it's a good thing Tim believes in God. Otherwise, with all the crap he gets from you he'd give up and go home. He couldn't survive in your existential void!"

Glynn snorted and we all went on with the game, laughing. Afterward I walked to the parking lot with this new comrade, Gus, wanting to know more about him. Raised in the Greek Orthodox church, he had attended seminary. With my very different Baptist upbringing, I wondered if we would end up arguing; instead, we discovered we shared many of the same spiritual yearnings.

What if neither of us had spoken up on the playing field? We never would have learned how much we had in common. Instead, we were able to celebrate our basic agreement as Christians, despite different traditions.

If others like Gus and me (whether Baptist or Catholic or Pentecostal) want to find any agreement or momentum, if they want to restore their sense of God's overarching will, they would do well to seek each other out and state their views. This doesn't mean becoming blind to differences. But it does mean being willing to talk, even to argue. Instead, Christians tend to take no position, for fear it will trap them or alienate others. And so they remain separated from one another, philosophically stranded.

A Bold Stance

Until we take a position and try to defend it, how can we get closer to being right? And how can we know we don't actually agree with those we thought were on "the other side"?

One of my favorite professors during my undergraduate years was a Roman Catholic. While visiting the University of Kansas for a semester, I was able to slip into a unique humanities program that Professor Senior was team-teaching along with a fellow Roman Catholic, Professor Quinn. The program was always on the verge of being axed due to controversy. The reason? The students kept converting to Catholicism.

Contrary to rumor, the two professors were not forcing students to become Catholics. They were simply not apologizing for their own religious beliefs or hiding them. Their candid, committed approach to truth was a wonderful reservoir in the desert of academic relativism. That's why all the conversions.

I remember well the class period when Professor Senior announced we would be reading sections of the Bible, even memorizing a psalm along with other poetry. He said, "If you have some objection, then we ask you to leave. We cannot possibly study Western civilization without taking a careful look at the Bible, the single most important influence in its formation." My soul sang out that day, because he was an honest and brave man.

There may have been a time when relativistic thought was daring, even revolutionary—when it was needed as an antidote to absolutist thought, a byproduct of fundamentalist Christianity. But now there's nothing radical about relativism. The ones who are radical are the ones like Professor Senior who still have the courage to say, "Some things are true for all of us."

Not that I always agreed with Professor Senior. We fought constantly over doctrinal issues. In fact, one day when I suggested that perhaps we weren't so far apart in our faith, Professor Senior replied, "On the contrary, our differences are so irreconcilable that undoubtedly one of us is going to hell."

Yet that didn't keep us from becoming friends. We wrote each other for several years afterward, and I was always amused to see how he signed his letters—"In *our* Savior's name."

That little pronoun—"our"—said a lot to me. Perhaps, after all, neither one of us is headed for hell.

Seven

Out of
Our Minds

BEFORE OUR WEDDING, CATHY AND I WENT THROUGH
four or five counseling sessions with our minister. They
were well worth the time. As the minister coaxed us into
dialogue, things we had felt but not put into words came floating to
the surface.

At the center of our meetings were two well-used psychological
tools: the Myers-Briggs personality profile and a diagnostic chart that
showed what kinds of family systems we had grown up in. When we
tallied the results, all three of us were fascinated. Could a thinking
introvert live with a feeling extrovert? Would a person from an open
family system get along with one from a more enmeshed family?

Each time we ventured further into this uncharted territory, we
came away intoxicated. We became so excited by our discoveries, in
fact, that we forgot something equally important. Prayer.

If we could pray with anyone, why not our minister? Yet for some
reason, we all three overlooked it.

No. I'll be more honest. I did not overlook it. I thought of it after
only one counseling session. But I was afraid to introduce the subject.
Our minister seemed so confident about the approach he was taking.
It was scientific—trustworthy. Prayer didn't seem necessary next to

it. Why consult a crystal ball when you *know* the future?

In this quiet way, psychology threatens the place of religion, sometimes even becoming a substitute for faith.

Where Psychology Has Never Gone

Today, more than ever, psychology sheds light on the dark places of the soul, making healing possible where it used to be unthinkable, introducing sensitivity and care where there used to be ruthlessness. Its importance is especially apparent in parts of the world where it is still not established as a valid method of treatment. There the consequences of mental disease are obvious and disconcerting.

When I was only seven, my family moved to Leimo, a mission station in Ethiopia, hundreds of miles south of the capital city of Addis Ababa. There, where our only connection with "civilization" was a thin red dirt road, psychology had not arrived—perhaps still hasn't—and we were reminded of that every time the local "crazy woman" came visiting.

We children spent our afternoons pushing yellow Tonka trucks across the dirt lawn and imitating the diesel engines that passed every few hours on the road to Addis. But if one of us heard the crazy woman wailing, we would drop our toys and scatter, racing for the nearest porch. Brave ones stayed there; the rest went inside and peeped out through windows. She would dash into the yard, half naked, her breasts bobbing and swinging. She would dart back and forth, unpredictable, hysterical, like a person chased by bees. One time, she grabbed a white sheet from our clothesline and galloped away with it half wrapped around her, a ghostly cape on her shoulders. We never saw that sheet again.

So terrifying was the crazy woman that I still know the Amharic word to describe her—*ibbed*. It ranks right up there next to the twenty or thirty other Amharic words I remember, next to "Hello" and "I'm hungry" and "Where's the bathroom?"

I have seen many *ibbed* people since then, in countries around the world. A lean, totally naked Kenyan chanting and springing up and down in the street, his hair powdered gray by dust and exhaust. Another naked man, this time sitting on a garbage heap outside a walled villa in the Philippines, staring out from under a bush of uncut hair. And yet another man, this time an American on a university campus, wearing only faded shorts, his back a huge cancerous scab. He is, for all I know, still making sudden little rushes, this way and that, only to return like a dog on a tether to the same worn spot, held there by some invisible power.

Who knows? Perhaps with treatment such people could be leading meaningful, productive lives. Maybe, in fact, that was the reason one Ethiopian family took the trouble to fly their *ibbed* son to Addis Ababa, twenty-five years ago, when we were still living at Leimo. We were going to Addis too. As we boarded the weekly DC-3 for the flight, we had to pass this *ibbed* man, who sat next to the door, restrained by his relatives. For some reason he didn't like my brother, who was only four then, and he kicked at him. Anytime Nat got near him, he rolled his eyes and swung his leg as if he were aiming at a soccer ball. It was terrifying for my brother to see an adult so bent on destroying him. It was terrifying for *me*.

Had his family heard of *psychology*? Was that why they were taking him to the city—perhaps hoping for a miracle?

It's likely. Psychology has that power—to bring the lost back, to restore to health, to save.

But so does faith, through prayer. And sometimes prayer applies more than psychology.

Spirit Is Not a Synonym for Psyche

Occasionally, I wake in the middle of the night convinced that there is something evil in the room. A wraithlike figure zooms toward me across the ceiling, face shrouded except for glinting eyes and a malevolent, open mouth. I throw my hands out to repel it. "Get out," I shout. "Now! In the name of Jesus, OUT."

That's when Cathy wakes and rolls over: "Tim?"

The figure is gone, but I am still stiff with adrenaline and struggling to understand.

"Tim. What was it?"

"I don't know. Something evil."

Is it a dream that spills over into real life, so vivid that it stays after I open my eyes? Is it car lights? (They do sometimes flash across the ceiling as a car turns into the nearby parking lot.) Or is it a spirit?

I don't *know*—can't know. But I *believe* that this is a *spirit*—an evil spirit.

The psychologist might wonder, "Don't you mean a 'projection'? Something that's a part of you—that you project into the room?"

No. Not *something,* but *someone.* And not from inside me, but from outside.

I'll admit that this unwanted visitor might be a product of my subconscious. But I insist that it might just as well be a spirit. Psychologists typically squirm at that thought, not to mention the thought that I might invoke another "spirit"—Jesus—to deal with the problem. But the weakness of psychology, in such matters, is that it is unavoidably introspective.

One of the great fathers of psychology, Carl Jung, insisted, "It is, to my mind, a fatal mistake to consider the human psyche as a merely personal affair and to explain it exclusively from a personal point of view."[1] He recognized that religious experience is essentially an experience of something "external to the individual"—a reality that transcends the individual.[2] But in practice, psychology rarely upholds such reality. It keeps life subjective, like a never-ending film that each of us is projecting out of our foreheads onto a screen.

I realize I am generalizing, but religion (by contrast to psychology) suggests that there is reality outside my self. Even those realities that seem private and subjective may come from outside me. My dreams are not necessarily manifestations of my inner state; they may be visions. Prayer is not just a way of ordering my private world; it is direct communication with God. And temptations? Those could be the influence of unseen powers outside myself.

The implication is that a whole realm of "principalities and powers" coexists with the world I know physically—a realm of spirits, holy and unholy. And those spirits may be revealed, fleetingly, with no explanation.

Granted, with my modern scientific mindset, that is hard to believe. I am uncomfortable with concepts that are not empirically verifiable. But if I am open-minded enough, I realize how well my skepticism might suit Satan, if indeed he does exist. It is to his advantage to have me doubt both him and God. It lets him exploit me without fear of discovery, and it keeps me from turning to God for discernment or aid.

C. S. Lewis captures this paradox brilliantly in his book *The Screwtape Letters*, wherein a senior devil advises a junior devil on how to maintain his hold over a human soul. Screwtape writes:

> My dear Wormwood, I wonder you should ask me whether it is essential to keep the patient in ignorance of your own existence. That question, at least for the present phase of the struggle, has been answered for us by the High Command. Our policy, for the moment, is to conceal ourselves. . . . When the humans disbelieve in our existence we lose all the pleasing results of direct terrorism. . . . On the other hand, when they believe in us, we cannot make them materialists and sceptics.[3]

I am not surprised that a certain school of psychology, disillusioned with Christianity, argues against spiritual reality. Members of this school of thought take the stance of Marx, the archskeptic who insisted that *real* happiness was possible only with the abolition of religion.[4] They feel that their task is to wean people from believing in the spiritual realm—to stop us from praying so that we can do "real" things about "real" problems.

They may have good reason for feeling this way. For instance, they may have experienced the unhealthy fear which is sometimes instilled in Christians by Christian leaders who twist prayer to their own ends.

But just because humans misrepresent God does not mean God is a myth. Give us humans time, and we will misrepresent anything. I have to remind myself of that, because I find I am easily influenced by the prevalent psychological theories about spiritual experience. Screwtape's line of argument is all too convincing. *Did I really feel God's presence? Or was it just wish fulfillment?* If I am not careful, I begin to explain away anything that seems spiritual. It's as if God were another tooth fairy and I should have outgrown my need for him by now.

I see others who struggle in the same way. One friend who has a doctorate in religious studies seemed intrigued when I told her about encountering the evil presence in our bedroom. When Cathy and I said we thought this spirit was trying to wear us down spiritually, she seemed to hear it differently than we meant.

In response, she described an eerie feeling she has when returning to her family home. "I don't even like to stay there overnight," she said, shivering at the thought. "There's too much psychic history. I can feel it when I step in the door—all the energy of our family's past, even the stuff that went on there before our family lived there."

What she was describing, as far as I could tell, was collective memories. Bad ones. Or some sort of abstract emotional residue. Probably not something capable of intelligent action, a personality with a will of its own. It seemed psychologically real, but not spiritually.

God Alone Knows!

The fact is, I'm in no position to prove what devils look like, or whether they even exist. More important, neither can I prove that God exists. I would be naive to think I could. But it is equally naive for me to believe that nothing exists except what my psyche brings into existence. The very fact that life was here before me and will go on after me is evidence that there are realities outside myself. If anyone is projecting those realities onto the screen of life—all the realities of creation—it is not me. It is God.

Sometimes I begin to act like God. After all, the world disappears on command when I close my eyes, and returns when I want it. Is it not mine to control?

But then everything becomes unmanageable. The sky cracks open and pours rain right when I want to play soccer. My grandmother's kidneys fail, and she is taken away, against my wishes. Or, to my surprise, I wake after a night with little sleep and I feel unusually rested, almost as if some outside power had been at work in me.

Who is in control of these surprises, both bad and good? I know that *I'm* not. And I suspect strongly that there is something going on around me, even in me, that is larger than me. I'm not convinced by the atheist's argument that just because I'm not in control, no one is in control. That seems short-sighted. To me it seems so much more likely that forces outside myself and stronger than myself are at work.

This is a critical issue to decide: whether or not God exists. If God is truly present—both omniscient and active—that reshapes everything about myself, including my sense of psychological well-being. If anyone knows what is truly healthy for me, God does. After all, God created me. My psyche too. So my health must be tied to my relationship with God.

In keeping with that premise, Scripture teaches that *because God first loved us* we can love others—not because we love ourselves. Yet how many times have I heard the reverse preached from the pulpit? How many times have I been encouraged simply to love myself, no matter how unlovable I might truly be? And how often have I heard ministers prescribing ways in which I can independently achieve happiness?

Positive thinker Robert Schuller has a whole book dedicated to this pursuit of happiness: *The Be (Happy) Attitudes.* "What we really have here," he says, "is a therapeutic exercise in replacing negative attitudes with positive attitudes."[5]

Now, I have nothing against happiness; I want happiness as much as the next person. And perhaps Schuller is a master of contextualization. He knows that our culture is highly psychological and obsessed with self-actualization. But I fear he is easily misunderstood. And the result, in my opinion, is a watered-down, weak gospel.

Did Jesus call people to be happy? When he said, "Come, take up your cross and follow me," was he calling people to happiness?

In some sense, yes. For he also said, "My yoke is easy and my burden is light" (Mt 11:30). But if I were to follow Christ only so that I could achieve happiness, I would not be truly following him, because he calls me first to surrender my personal motives and desires. That is the true beginning of whatever happiness God offers.

Paradoxically, psychological health (or happiness) is based on being set free from the very thing we think we need. "Go, sell everything you have and give to the poor," Jesus said to the rich man (Mk 10:21). Likewise, when I come to him, Jesus may begin by saying, "Give up your most cherished need—this need for happiness, for personal comfort. Turn it over to me, in prayer, and I will care for you."

He wants me to be free too. He wants all people to be free.

When we have released our need, then if we are given the things we sought, we are all the more happy. But if we are not given what we sought, we are still happy. We are at peace either way. Like the apostle Paul, we can say that we have learned the secret of being content, "whether living in plenty or in want" (Phil 4:12).

The fact is that those who *do* follow Jesus find joy that is even deeper and more stable than what they call happiness. They become people who love themselves. They earn their own respect. But the starting place is their commitment to his challenging call, their willingness to obey. In that sense, psychological healing is a byproduct of first of all "doing the right thing," obeying God's rules. Healthy rules. The very source of joy.

Twelve Steps to God

I know two wonderful artists, both of them from painfully dysfunctional families. David and Marilyn would have destroyed themselves utterly—they nearly did—in an attempt to find happiness. They were products of the sixties. They barely survived the seventies, wandering across the nation in a van, while David slowly turned to drugs, chasing the illusion of finding happiness in experiences. They traveled here and there, trying to love each other but failing, becoming more lost, more unhappy, more destructive. Then, after they had separated (because they could not love each other enough to live together) both of them discovered God.

Marilyn, through prayer, experienced sudden healing from a circulatory illness which at one point had nearly taken her life. And David found himself mysteriously led into a coffee house, to work for a Christian man who decided he must give David a job even if he couldn't think of a job to give him. Eventually David, too, became a Christian, and through prayer he miraculously lost his need for drugs.

Today, David and Marilyn are two of the most sane and loving people I know. The way I know they are sane is that they would laugh at me if I said this to their faces. They are happy in the fullest sense. God has brought them out of their dying selves into life, into health. God has given them reason to love. They tracked each other down again after becoming Christians, married, and began a new life together, one which has now lasted twelve years.

To me they are a testimony that psychological self-interest can get us only so far. To be fully set free we must arrive at a place where God's existence is clear and his pleasure is more important than ours. We must be able to pray, believing that God hears and answers.

And yet, in the context of their newfound faith, psychology has been an important means for further healing. Both David and Marilyn have been through therapy on and off over the past fifteen years, and they always find it rejuvenating. Marilyn says, in fact, that she meets very committed Christians who scare her because they have done so little to understand themselves or to find healing. For her, therapy has been a bit like taking a lamp into a dark cave and discovering all sorts of hidden things—both treasures and monsters. She has had to face the monsters to recover what was rightfully hers. She has had to feel new feelings. And through this process she has begun to live more fully.

David and Marilyn don't see psychology and faith as being at odds. They have especially high regard for the twelve-step Adult Children of Alcoholics program. Without their ACOA therapy group, they feel they would have remained stunted in their personal growth. They point out, though, that the starting point for all twelve-step recovery programs is really a spiritual confession in three parts, as originally formulated for Alcoholics Anonymous:

1. We admitted we were powerless over alcohol—that our lives had become unmanageable.

2. We came to believe that a Power greater than ourselves could restore us to sanity.

3. We made a decision to turn our will and our lives over to the care of God as we understood Him.[6]

David and Marilyn say that members of a twelve-step program may quibble over the definition of "greater Power," but at rock bottom, this successful therapeutic system is still based on the assumption that the self is not the highest power in the universe. To find healing, each person must submit to a higher power. Indeed, Christians who have the courage to say these words realize that they are actually praying, "Yes, Lord, I will follow you."

Going Public!

Separate the two, psychology and religion, and you get either uninspired logic or misguided superstition. But together they are complete.

The only remaining factor is the community.

Try to imagine, if you can, the twelve-step therapy program working without community. It's impossible. Without community, there would be no support and no accountability. The proclamations of the people involved would be just words. That's because what empowers those words is the fact that they are public. In effect, they are a confession! Once stated, they naturally lead to repentance and change, because they have been witnessed. The person is compelled, by going public, to start over. And the person is able to do this because the community empathizes and encourages, offering constant support.

One doesn't have to be part of a formal therapy group to experience therapy. We can build therapeutic communities that help us to understand ourselves and improve. Cathy and I have met with our friends David and Marilyn for over three years, intentionally sharing what we are experiencing as individuals and as couples. We talk a lot about our work and about gifts. We also talk about our relationships as couples. And we often close with prayer, focusing very directly on each other's needs. We are sort of a therapy group, and at the same time sort of a church. We are a Christian community seeking health with God's help.

On occasion, Cathy and I are afraid to meet with these wonderful friends because we have been fighting or we are depressed. We know it will be impossible for us to hide that, and we're embarrassed. But once we force ourselves to enter into relationship with them, we experience healing. No matter how painful the encounter, we don't regret it. Somehow, the very act of being public with our difficulty defuses it; our friends accept us, sins and all. They help us find forgiveness and assure us we're not hopeless; and prayer helps us to go back to living with new hope and peace. On those difficult occasions, we may storm into the room nearly choked with resentment or rage or sorrow, but by the time we leave we are able once again to face life, breathing deeply. We go into the room crazy but come out sane.

Ibbed people are loners. It's hard to say which comes first, being cut off or being crazy, but the two are definitely related. For that reason, anything we can do to live in relationship helps prevent illness—that is, if we build healthy relationships, through honesty and prayer. In certain situations there will be no substitute for professional counseling, particularly if we are trapped without healthy relationships. But in our search for inner healing, we should never overlook the guidance possible in healthy relationships. We can build communities that we trust, with God's help.

And there is no better place to start than in the home—with our wife or husband.

Next stop? Sex.

Eight

Safe for
Sex

O NE DAY IN COLLEGE, I LISTENED UNEASILY AS A FRIEND
described her sister's ordination. She was uneasy too, so
uneasy that she had written a term paper on the ordination
of women. Her conclusion? It was doctrinally sound. Clearance granted.

We argued back and forth like good college students, and I realized
I had never considered women as ministers. In the circles where I
grew up, which included a lot of conservative Christians, women's
ordination was not a popular concept. And the church our family had
returned to from Africa didn't allow women to take any leadership.
They rarely stood on the platform unless they were in the choir. If
one of them took the pulpit for a solo, even then the minister hovered
close at hand, in case the microphone went to her head.

My parents didn't have such hangups. In fact, in early adulthood
I learned that after becoming a Christian, my mother's first desire was
to go to seminary. She didn't go, but she might as well have, for all
the public speaking and ministering she's done since.

As for me, I ended up in love with a woman suspiciously like my
mother. To the surprise of everyone (except perhaps my mother), I
eventually proposed to this woman, who was in seminary and deter-

mined to get ordained. That's how I ended up in downtown Chicago on December 15, 1991, watching Cathy lie face down before the bishop as a sign of her submission to Christ and to the church.

My childhood church had planted the idea that my wife should lie down in submission to *me,* not the church, so this was a bit unsettling to watch, but it was right. It put things in perspective.

I remember that after I entered the cathedral that day, once I stopped worrying about where to take the in-laws for dinner, I was surprised. I had expected one of those dark Gothic interiors that Episcopalians are so fond of. Instead, the space felt bright and airy. Byzantine. Like one of the early Eastern churches. And that seemed fitting.

I have always thought of the fifth- and sixth-century Byzantine Christians as immensely committed. To become a Christian then, let alone to become a priest, required a lengthy period of training and testing—up to three years. Cathy had shown just as much commitment, fighting through a gauntlet of committees and bishops and professors, all armed with tests designed to stop the uncalled and let only the remnant through. Her ordination represented to me the fitting culmination of this difficult period of preparation. It was the long-awaited seal of approval.

What were they approving? Her gifts. Together, they were saying, "We've looked and looked at you and tried to find any reason why you couldn't do this work—and we've tried to strengthen you where you needed it—and now we all agree. You are gifted to be a priest."

I agreed, too, having watched her through the process. If Cathy was made in God's image as much as I was, and if God was calling her to use the gifts he had given her, then who was I to stand in the way? None of the old hesitations remained. If I struggled at all, it was only because, to be honest, I had a tinge of envy. I thought, *Wouldn't it be nice if I could get ordained?*

I believe we all long to have our gifts recognized and blessed. We want to be called. And in that sense God wants us to be ordained.

Ordained as men. Ordained as women. Ordained to live out our gifts in relationship to each other.

The trick here is that to live out our gifts we *must* live relationally. Modern societies aren't big on relationships. Sex, yes! But relationships . . . ?

Sex, Madonna Style

To illustrate, let me leap across the Atlantic, back to Africa. What do you imagine is one of the most popular types of TV programming across Africa?

Rock videos.

At an outdoor cafe in Côte d'Ivoire, I found myself watching a TV set that had been hung on the wall, apparently to draw bored diners like myself. There was Madonna, belly-dancing her way through another of her intentionally shocking rock extravaganzas. Then I noticed two African men off to the side, leaning against a wall. Judging by their intense concentration, they weren't there to eat. They were there for the show. That wouldn't have meant much to me, except that I could tell by their white robes and fezzes that they were Muslim.

In Islamic Africa, husbands and wives don't touch each other in public. Everyone dresses to protect, not to reveal. But there they stood, transfixed by this semi-naked, pelvis-thrusting, moaning sex goddess. Staring. Staring. Saying nothing to each other. I became so unsettled, watching them, that I couldn't enjoy the rest of my meal.

I have become relatively immune to sexual explicitness. At least I try to be. Sexuality is so pervasive here that I have to ignore it or it will consume all my attention. When I commute to work, I am likely to be confronted daily by huge billboard women dressed in nothing but pantyhose or flowing hair—or a perfectly molded man, lounging in his underwear. There they are, lined up for the visual taking. Or when I go to a film, I am almost certain to see a man and a woman—usually hardly introduced, much less married—falling into bed locked in a tight embrace.

These gods and goddesses seem to enjoy a freedom sexually that knows no limits. Like Madonna, they get as much sex as they can, wherever they can. And so, though I try to remain unaffected, I sometimes crave that same freedom. I want in on it.

That's a major problem—because I can't live that way. It's an illusion. Even Madonna can't find the freedom she portrays in her videos and films—I'd bet on that. Sexual partners don't just come and go at our whims. They don't just fall into our arms when we want them, attracted by newly brushed teeth or a new cologne.

Everything I have learned of sex tells me that it is inescapably relational. Even if it lasts for only a night, it is relational. And that is why it can't possibly work as easily as it does on the movie screen. Whenever there is a relationship, there can't be complete freedom. Eventually the two will disagree, run up against different expectations, get frustrated. Being male or female is more complicated and difficult than that. It takes commitment, not just desire.

By letting go of Cathy on the day of her ordination, and by trying to see her in relationship to God (who was calling her to do something special), I was able to live in even better relationship with her. By supporting her as she searched for a job she would enjoy, and by "following" her to a new church, I was able to grow in my love for her. But that took commitment, not just desire.

I'll admit it: It wasn't easy.

Actually, we fought desperately when she went looking for a position. She wanted to interview anywhere: New York, California, Texas, Kenya, you name it. She insisted, with a frantic look in her eye, "Look, it's not easy getting a place as a woman priest. It may not work out right here where we are."

But I didn't want to move. I liked my Chicago-based job, training writers and editors in the Third World. And, as I pointed out to her, it wasn't easy to find a job like that just *anywhere*. When she kept pushing, I took the silent approach: don't talk about it and maybe it will go away.

One evening we had a phone conversation with friends. Cathy was talking excitedly about a lead that had surfaced in San Francisco. I fell silent, hoping that they would all pack it up and put it away— just forget it.

"So what about you, Tim? What are the job options if you end up in San Francisco?" our friends asked.

"I'm not looking," I replied. "I like it right here."

There was a long pause. Then the conversation went on, everyone trying to overlook my reaction. By the time we got off the phone, it had sunk in. I finally had to admit that I hadn't been willing to see things from Cathy's perspective. What if God really did have something special in mind for her (not to mention myself)? What if he had been preparing her all through seminary to do a very particular work somewhere else? I realized reluctantly that I hadn't been living in relationship with her, or with God, just with myself.

That was when I let go and began to listen to Cathy seriously. As she described her possibilities and what attracted her to one place over another, I began to explore with her how her gifts might fit. I visited one or two places with her. I even talked with my boss, who said that if we had to go, he would let me work for the company from a distance.

Then the miracle happened: A position opened at a church only twenty miles from where we lived. Not only was it near, but it seemed to fit the gifts Cathy had to offer. And she actually wanted the position!

I couldn't believe it. By the time this church asked Cathy to become an assistant priest, I had become so used to the thought of leaving the state that I even felt regret. *Now that I'm ready to go, we aren't going!*

We stayed, and I learned my lesson: to respect Cathy's call from God. And I learned to think more relationally. I saw that our call to each other was just as important as—or more important than—our calls to our separate careers.

Blazing the Sexual Trail

In reality, Westerners have much to be proud of when it comes to sexual freedom. No matter how much further we may need to liberate ourselves—not only as women, but also as men—we have already gone further than most people worldwide. In many less-developed countries, there are places where a woman will marry the man she is given to, bear children on demand, work in the fields like an ox, eat silently after her husband has taken the best food, never voice an opinion except to other women, and die virtually unknown.

Over and over I have visited such places and have been silently served by my host's wife, who disappeared to eat separately. And I have wondered, *What is she thinking? What could she add to this conversation that I am missing?*

Those of us from sexually liberated societies have much to offer in places like that.

But we are still learning, and learning is never easy. As we forge ahead, cutting the path for those who follow, we sometimes find ourselves lost. The changing terrain bewilders—makes us tense, defensive. The old roles were at least comfortable and familiar. Now that they are no longer appropriate, what is to replace them? Where to go next?

When Cathy and I married it was like creatures from separate planets moving in with one another. I had been raised on a masculine planet, where my mother was outnumbered four-to-one by a husband and three sons. Burping contests were common. Cathy had been raised on a feminine planet, where her dad played solo male to a wife and four daughters. Burping was not an accepted form of communication. Not surprisingly, she and I found each other mysterious, sometimes maddening.

Why is it so important, Cathy wondered, *that we go camping together? Why does he blame me for not being willing to hike for days on end without a shower?*

I, on the other hand, wondered, *What is it about drinking imported coffee together, or showing interest in scones, that makes her so happy?*

We lived out a crosscultural adventure that surpassed anything I had experienced before. Sometimes we still do.

The hardest part for Cathy and me is not the expectations we place on each other, but the expectations we place on ourselves. Early in our marriage, she automatically took on the burden of housecleaning because that was "woman's work," and she suffered guilt when she felt she was not as good a housekeeper as her mother. I took on things like getting the oil changed in the car and paying the bills. I wished that she would do some of it, but I never voiced that desire because, after all, it was really "man's work." Over and over, we got upset at each other, not because we expected the other person to do the work, but because we couldn't stop doing it ourselves.

It's hard to break old patterns. A rolling train can't easily be directed off its tracks. So I feel fortunate that my father was in the home much more than my grandfather, and that he was actively involved in raising us. I am glad that I saw him now and then with soapsuds on his hands. That has made it easier for me to stand in the same place, in front of heaps and heaps of dishes, doing my part in the household.

And yet the patterning is still there to wrestle with. It is easy for me to let Cathy vacuum the floors and do the laundry, even when she has put in a longer work week than I have; she does it automatically, and besides, that was always my mother's work. I have to make myself offer to help. Otherwise the train goes careening down the same old track, headed for the same destination.

To make matters worse, the church hasn't exactly leaped out to show the way. Since the old roles were carefully buttressed by selective biblical references, they resist being restructured. My attempts to take the advice of the apostle Paul in his letter to the Ephesians—to love my wife as myself—are countered by those who cling to Paul's words in the same passage about submission (Eph 5:22-33). From their vantage point, you would think that if Cathy disagrees with me, I should force her to her knees in obedience to me.

That's loving her as myself? If so, then no wonder young Christian men and women feel confused or cynical. No wonder, either, that some Christian women are leaving the church. They go away complaining that the church is a closed system of patriarchy, dominated by male language, male thinking, male leadership—and I don't blame them. If I went to a meeting where the only pronouns used were feminine, I might feel the same way. Especially if I was told (always by women leaders) that the meeting would help me to deal with my experience *as a man.*

The question, then, is this: Can there be a new way to be Christian and female? To be Christian and male? If Paul was right—that in Christ there is neither Jew nor Greek, slave nor free, male nor female (Gal 3:28)—then how can we live out that balance? There's enough different about men and women, both physically and experientially, to give us different strengths and weaknesses, but what can we do to find out who we are and to complement each other rather than wrestling for control?

Virginity Isn't an Accident

You can't really talk about sexual roles without talking about sex itself. It's all too interwoven. So I'll admit it: when it came to sex, Cathy and I were dinosaurs. We were part of that threatened species who enter marriage as virgins. And that has a lot to do with the way we live out our sexual roles now.

Our virginity didn't just happen. It took a lot of effort. At times it felt like self-inflicted torture. I remember, in particular, a muggy evening when we stood on the dark veranda of my apartment as one of those wonderful Midwestern storms rolled in over the plains. The rain clouds broke, bathing us in a gentle shower. A breeze loosened the night. And suddenly Cathy's dress seemed indescribably thin between us. My hands were so yearning that I couldn't resist baring one of her breasts, touching her there, kissing her. Then somehow we stopped, as if in agreement that someday this would continue.

As I have watched friends (so many of them) choose to go the other way, I have wondered if our society has changed so much that the standards of Christianity must change to match it. I have felt Cathy and I are out of sync—museum pieces. With all the sexual encouragement American youth receive, how can we expect them to act differently? If commitment is impossible, why shouldn't they go ahead and get what they can?

Still, I am glad I chose over and over again not to give in to my desires. And I am glad Cathy made the same difficult choice. We are free now in a way that I never could have imagined. We are free of the scars, the disfigured memories, the psychological baggage that I have seen others carry. No former lover creeps into bed with us when we make love, raising comparisons or feelings of guilt. And there's no reason for us to doubt we can stay true to each other. We already have.

As a result, we trust each other not just in bed but in those everyday decisions that could so easily make us go to war. We trust each other in splitting the household chores, in deciding how we will plan a career change, in talking with friends of the opposite sex. Trust is the bedrock on which we build. And that trust began with our conscious effort to respect each other enough *not* to make love—not until there was solid commitment between us.

Being a virgin at marriage may not be a prerequisite for a good marriage, but honest and faithful commitment is. That I know. One couple lived together for years before marriage, but when they became Christians they recognized the need to prove their commitment to each other. They stopped making love for a period of six months before getting married. It was their way to start over, sanctifying the experience of marriage. And it was their way of making sure that their relationship was built on more than sexual need. It must have been, because they are still married, and lovingly, over ten years later.

Good Sex and God

Freedom is wonderful. We all want it. But true freedom on a sexual level is possible only with security. And security comes from commitment. Commitment to each other. To the relationship itself. To God.

The latter has been especially important for Cathy and me. Without commitment to God, our human efforts at love are incomplete. We are finite and selfish by nature. But God is infinite and utterly just. He can bring us the fairness we are looking for—if we are only willing to commit ourselves to him. As a result, Cathy and I try to pray constantly about our sexuality, thanking God for it, asking him to bless it and to help us, as a man and a woman, to live out our sexuality in a way that will glorify him.

Before meeting Cathy, I had prayed for years that God would help me find the right woman to marry. One winter night in graduate school, after yet another romance had collapsed, I prayed my way out into a dark, frozen field, crunching bitterly through the tall grass. I lay down in that icy wasteland, breathing frost into the air, and literally shouted at God, "Why? Why not now? Am I never going to find someone I can live with?"

As I look back, I realize that God saved that other woman and me from disaster, a disaster that we could not have avoided if we had ignored the signals he was sending, if we had just followed our urges.

Not long afterward, God introduced me to Cathy, the woman I had been looking for—whom I could love fairly, equally, honestly. He provided. And now, whenever we feel conflict rising up between us, Cathy and I force ourselves to look outside, back to God. God keeps providing the balance that we couldn't find on our own. With his help, Cathy and I are finding "sexual freedom." Freedom to live out our gifts fully. And freedom to express ourselves sexually.

From the beginning I felt this sexual freedom unfolding in our marriage. Before the honeymoon, to be honest, I feared that mysterious and mythic night when I would lie down to discover and to be discovered. I trembled at the thought of such complete vulnerability. Never could I have imagined how at ease I would feel. How free.

I'll admit, I have nothing to compare it with. But that's exactly why I am so confident about it. When Cathy and I discovered sex, we did it as if no one had ever discovered it before. We were the first! And to some extent, we remain the first: forging ahead, discovering unique joys that no one else has discovered or will discover. And we celebrate together, because by God's grace we were able to protect and enjoy that precious freedom.

What I am talking about is not the anarchic, momentary nonsense that Madonna presents. As I watch that "freedom" being broadcast across the world, I fear what it will do to those who watch. I especially fear for the children—the next generation of married couples.

I think of a five-year-old Kenyan girl and her eight-year-old sister, staring at MTV in their Nairobi home, their parents oblivious or too busy to notice the rock videos they were watching. It was a relatively progressive home, although the father still held to some strong conservative values. As we talked, he admitted that he struggled with the concept of women's liberation. "It's all right for you. In America you can do anything. But here?"

He struggled honestly, in a battle that I believe he will let himself lose some day. He will see the dignity of those he battles against, his wife and daughters included. But what worries me is that he seemed utterly blind that evening to another battle, one which is probably going on inside his children nightly as they learn from women and men who do not know their own dignity, who have confused liberation with self-indulgence.

Those children, whom he is trying so hard to guide, are being encouraged by almost every rock video to grow into women who do as they please, without any thought for the other person, without any commitment. Right now they are building their future, and they are building on illusions. When they have finished building what they thought was a palace, will they find instead that it is a cage?

Let us find ways to help all children—the next generation—to learn how to be sexual beings freely, in true relationship to each other and to God. Let's talk about it all—and openly.

Nine

Rescued
from Success

THE PURITAN LEADER JOHN WINTHROP PREACHED TO THE
Pilgrims halfway across the Atlantic Ocean, challenging
them to succeed for Christ's sake. He rallied them together
in a most eloquent speech, claiming that if they succeeded, they would
become a model for all others to follow: "For we must consider that
we shall be as a city upon a hill. The eyes of all people are upon us."[1]

As the Puritans landed at Plymouth Rock full of hope and deter-
mination, the American drive for progress was deeply reinforced by
religion. In effect, it became "Christian" to succeed.

Out of fairness to Winthrop, we should note that he *had* to call the
Puritans to success. He was their leader, and he knew how likely it
was that their grand experiment would end in disaster. Also, Winthrop never said that the Pilgrims should succeed for their own sake,
but for God's sake. He believed that if they failed, that would reflect
on God: "if we . . . shall fail to embrace this present world and prose-
cute our carnal intentions, seeking great things for ourselves and our
posterity, the Lord will surely break out in wrath against us."[2]

Winthrop did what he could to warn the Puritans against the
dangers of success, while still calling for success. It was as if, even
then, he could see in their eyes the deep subterranean need to be

known, to be recognized for accomplishing something *big*. Indeed, they were people with dreams, so they carried on, and they *did* succeed. And because they were Christians, they welded their dreams to their faith. The alloy that was formed was that peculiar thing sometimes labeled "the Protestant work ethic." We have been living with it ever since.

A Successful Society?

An African visitor had been in the U.S. for a month when I asked what had surprised him most.

"Oh!" he said, "It was the first day I visited a grocery store." I nodded, assuming that he had been shocked by the great variety of products. Instead, he added, "I couldn't believe how quickly the clerk put the groceries in the bag."

Today, centuries after the Puritans, Americans still work even when they don't feel like it. That's because, like the Puritans, they believe in progress. No matter how menial or difficult the work, work can lead to better things.

People from other countries with a strong Reformation heritage, such as Germany, have the same optimistic faith in work. This ethic has carried them far. Because they believe progress is possible, they succeed. And what a wonderful gift—to succeed. People from many cultures haven't had the opportunity to make such progress and so they are fatalistic.

Take Eastern Europeans. Prior to the fall of Marxism, their approach to work shocked visitors. One said he enjoyed going into Romanian shops about as much as running into a wall. The clerks just stared at him. He had to practically beg them to get things from behind the counter so that he could look at them.

But what incentive was there for helping him? With everything state-controlled, they would not lose their jobs by ignoring him. And they could not advance by working harder. So why do anything?

A story is going around lately about an idealistic corporate manager from Eastern Europe who visited the U.S. soon after the Berlin Wall came down. He was hoping to seal a joint venture with a U.S. corporation. During dinner, at the home of his new business partner, he insisted that his host explain the finer points of free enterprise. But at the end of the evening, while saying goodby, he asked, "Now tell me, just one more time—why do we have to make a profit?"

In a free-enterprise state we take the answer for granted. People are expected to be productive, no matter what they do. They are expected to make a profit. People in the middle and upper classes are particularly optimistic. They usually have a history of family success to stand on. And they have the resources to move forward. So they believe in themselves. Driving forward with sheer willpower, they accomplish the impossible. As a result, they have an energetic beauty.

The rest of the world—watching as my African friend watched the busy grocery clerk—is entranced by this energy and confidence. Note the fascination worldwide with U.S. movies, rock music and athletics. Through such entertainment, American culture itself (built on the myth of personal success) has become the U.S.'s biggest export.

But the rest of the world is not only fascinated; sometimes it is resentful.

Ambition Bites Back
For the outsider, it is almost frightening how confident and driven Americans are. On entry to the U.S., visitors can feel they must be active or get lost. And sometimes that is just what Americans demand: either do something or leave.

Take a look at our corporate heroes—men like Ted Turner, *Time*'s man of the year for 1991. On Turner's desk rests a plaque with this popular saying: "Lead, follow, or get out of the way." He has brought to life the American dream, and he didn't get there by being nice.

And yet, Ted Turner has lived with a bogey monster. Over the years, he has feared that he would kill himself—just as his father did when Turner was a child.

Turner's father was so determined to instill in him a passion for success that he demanded the boy read two books each week. If he failed, he was punished. So Turner learned well. Like F. Scott Fitzgerald's character Gatsby, he became driven toward success. Just as surely as Gatsby yearned to reach the green light across the bay, so full of promise, Turner yearned for his own form of success. And like Gatsby, Turner felt so driven toward his goals that he risked destroying himself with effort and anxiety. That is why he has struggled for much of his adult life with the fear that he would someday kill himself.[3]

But Turner isn't that unusual. People everywhere, Christians included, run the same risk, even if it is more metaphoric, when they buy into the success myth. Success will not necessarily lead to satisfaction. It can enslave us or even destroy us, unless we put it in relationship to the overarching will of God.

Goals in Collision

John, a young financial manager who is now a member of our church, had a revolutionary shift in his understanding of success. For years he had been chasing the dream: going to the right schools, finding the right job, buying a house in the right suburb, slowly building what we call "the good life." But he couldn't get rid of a nagging sense of dissatisfaction. One day on his way to work, he flipped on the radio and happened to get a Christian station. He turned it off when he realized it was one of "those stations." Then he turned it back on, curious. He realized that he really *did* want to think more about his faith.

After that, John began to listen to the program regularly. His car radio broke; he put a portable radio in his car so he could keep listening. But that very day, as he was turning left, another car ran through a stoplight and smashed into his car.

Rather than being distracted by the accident, John had a sudden sense that someone was trying to keep him from listening to the radio program. And he realized that what he really wanted in life was to be more like Christ. As he waited at the gas station for his car to be towed, he found himself handing out cookies his wife had sent to work with him. "It was wonderful," he said. "The most enjoyable thing I had done in years. I decided I could hand out cookies for a living. That would be enough. Just to hand out cookies."

When eventually John came to terms with what he was experiencing, he wrote a letter to all the members of his family. It began: "Moving to Deerfield signified for me the fulfillment of a number of my life goals. I had a wonderful wife, a good job, a house in a nice area. I was entering the final year of classes for my MBA from one of the top business schools and looking forward to starting a family. I should have been happy. I had a lot more than most people in this world and more than the average American. But I was not happy! I had felt for quite a while that there was something missing from my life. I had hoped that this emptiness would be filled by attaining my life goals, but it was still there."

He went on to explain about the Christian radio station, and about a booklet he had read when he was in bed with a cold—along with the Gospel of John and other parts of the Bible. It was after reading those Bible passages that he had finally and willfully committed himself to Christ, asking to follow Christ as his disciple.

"Probably at this point you think I have gone completely bonkers," he wrote to his family, "but actually I have never had so much inner peace in my life as I have had since my day of decision. What does all this mean for my life on earth? Well, only God knows, but so far I am reading the Bible and praying daily. I am learning what God requires of Christians, and I am working toward loving my neighbors as I love myself. My life is his and I am here to do his will."

What a radical shift! John had been driven to accomplish some vague goal. He had worked to keep up with all the others, never knowing why. But suddenly, instead of living to reach his own goals, he wanted to live to reach God's goals.

Interestingly, John had gone to church all his life. He knew the Nicene Creed by heart. He had been successful as a "Christian." Now, for the first time, he realized what it meant to be Christlike. He claimed the words of the creed as he said them anew, "We believe in one Lord, Jesus Christ, the only Son of God. ... Through him all things were made. For us and for our salvation he came down from heaven."[4] With the shift in his priorities, John was able to confess the Christian faith with conviction.

Called to Succeed?

When John shared his family letter with me, I thought, *It seems so simple. Then why is it so hard to do? Why do I struggle to give up my own drivenness even after years of carefully defining my faith against the backdrop of the convenience culture?*

Then I began to wonder: *Could it be that my Christianity is so infected with the need for success-at-any-price that I am not even conscious how I have redefined "being Christian"?*

A decade ago, when I was a student at Wheaton College, that Vatican of evangelicalism, famous Christians were paraded in front of me daily on the chapel stage: Billy Graham, J. I. Packer, Chuck Colson, rock star Phil Keaggy, a Christian lawyer from Wall Street, a Christian corporation owner, Christian heroes of a hundred varieties.

What is a young person supposed to think if those are always the models of Christianity—if being Christian is presented in the same way as "Entertainment Tonight"? For me the natural conclusion was that every Christian should accomplish as much. Go to the Senate, publish a bestseller, appear on screen, rise to the top. Anything less was failure. And failure was taboo.

Looking back now, I know those evangelical "heroes" weren't there to tell me I should be famous. The fact is that most Christian heroes do not become heroes because they want to be. If you aim at success for success's sake, then when people get in the way you must push them aside or give up your goal (neither of which is very Christlike).

And yet that was the message I received: that success was the goal. I learned it from the way those heroes were treated—the adulation that was given to them. And I learned it from the lack of models who were not "famous."

Granted, Jesus was famous. But he was notorious for stopping so that he could take care of people. He stopped for folks who showed faith, regardless of their popularity or potential. Then, when he went on, he took them with him. They went together with him, and they became stronger, healthier people along the journey.

Today, many African Christians still live out Jesus' way. Some disparage themselves for being unable to meet on time or to make things happen quickly. They believe what the textbooks teach: that they are part of an undeveloped country and therefore *they* are undeveloped. But development occurs on many levels. Though they may not get to their destinations as quickly as people in the First World, these African Christians take others with them. They readily stop the truck to pick up people who don't have a vehicle. They stop again just to talk, even though they have an errand to run and even though the people in back are waiting. They take a cousin into their home for the next two years so that she can go to a better school. They won't sacrifice the progress of others for their own progress.

When I see it that way, I have to redefine *development*. Being busy or productive is only one dimension of social development, and no nation is truly developed if its success is obtained at the expense of others.

Of course, on the other hand, Christians from countries labeled "undeveloped" are not automatically saints. It's easy to be generous for the wrong reasons: out of peer pressure, out of the desire to be liked or a lack of personal purpose. In the end, we must all be motivated spiritually, not by what our culture expects of us.

For all Christians, regardless of nationality, all goals must be assessed in the light of God's goals: "Thy Kingdom come, thy will be done." After years of praying those words, it is still hard for me to comprehend what I mean. I'm still learning. But it seems that if I am sincere, I have to be willing to live like Jesus. Acting out God's will, he took up a basin of water and washed feet, becoming a servant.

A servant? What is that? Since today's democratic societies aren't big on servants or footwashing, we may have to do some translation work. When I try, I come up with this translation: *Maybe I must find ways to regularly help other people reach their goals. Maybe, since I am so easily sucked into self-interest, I need to discipline myself to do at least one thing each week for someone else in need.*

In my case, for awhile it was tutoring Hispanic children. One year it was visiting a minimum-security prison for juvenile delinquents, going each week to help give them a Sunday service. But the options are limitless. I could visit a nursing home (as one group from my church does). I could volunteer time at a city shelter. I could even babysit for someone who needs time away from the kids. I just need to do something that someone else needs, to remind myself that my own success is not paramount.

A Wise Foolishness

I like Jimmy Carter. For all the criticism he received as president, he has certainly proved himself to be Christlike in his leadership. Today, he travels from country to country trying to bring leaders together to resolve conflicts—to reach their goals, not his. And at home, he regularly straps on a carpenter's belt and climbs onto a scaffold to help build homes for the homeless. He gives time for their good, not his own.

In the eyes of a success-driven person, such action may seem foolish. There are better things to do with one's time, just as there are better things to do after a car wreck than to hand out cookies. But the wisdom of God is foolishness, until we risk it. Then suddenly it makes sense!

I have learned that without such perspective, I risk becoming either an obsessive, solitary workaholic or a defeatist. But when I put my efforts into relationship with others and especially with God, work becomes meaningful, satisfying. I am set free from having to be successful.

The only other vital ingredient is love. "If I give all I possess to the poor and surrender my body to the flames, but have not love, I gain nothing" (1 Cor 13:3).

Love should fuel all my efforts. Why? Because otherwise I will still be motivated by my own need for success. At the back of *true* success (which is God's success) is a love which does everything in utter freedom and purity.

Love is what we all lost at the Fall, and it is what I must regain, with God's help. It is so easy to do things for my own selfish reasons—even good things. As Winthrop explained while the Mayflower plowed its way toward the New World: "But Adam rent himself from his creator, rent all his posterity all so one from another; whence it comes that every man is born with this principle in him, to love and seek himself only, and thus a man continueth 'til Christ comes and takes possession of the soul and infuseth another principle, love to God and our brother."[5]

Winthrop recognized that real love looks outward. I don't always feel this love when I want to. But if I offer myself to Christ—to let him "take possession of the soul"—I discover that love follows, both toward him and toward others. And then I am set free to enjoy life, no matter what my circumstances. I do not even need success.

Ten

Time
Release

I AM ONE OF THOSE PEOPLE WHO ALWAYS NEEDS TO BE PRO-
ductive. I come home from work with a list of scheduled events.
If they are thrown off by a flat tire or a sudden visitor, I'm
upset.

Take an all-too-typical scenario. Finished with work on Wednesday, I jump in my car. Normally I would go straight home, which
takes fifty minutes, but this day I have a counseling session and that
means an even longer drive. I'm late because I worked overtime, so
I drive seventy. I try not to feel guilty. *After all, everyone else is
driving eighty. You almost risk having an accident by driving slower.*

As I drive, I whip out my hand-size tape recorder to dictate a letter.
Late or not, why waste the time? Then I discover I'm almost out of gas.
I'll have to stop at the roadside oasis, since I don't have time to exit
the highway. I fill up at the self-serve island, then pay by using a
gadget on the pump which takes credit cards. *A little time saved.*

Though I'm late, I'm also hungry, and there's a McDonald's next to
the station. I've eaten so many hamburgers lately that I get a stale
greasy taste in my mouth just thinking about them, but when else am
I going to eat? I've got a soccer game right after the session. And if

I wait to cook something at home, at nine o'clock, I won't have any time for writing. I groan: *I had really hoped to do a bit of writing tonight.*

I begin running across the parking lot, then realize I'm out of cash. *Now what?*

I remember there's an automatic cash machine inside, so I dash into McDonald's and plug in my card. The machine spits out a bunch of bills.

Uh-oh, a school bus must have just emptied. At least five people in each line. I wait impatiently in one line, then switch to another. *They call this "fast"?* When I get the food, I run for the car.

I could pray. Try to calm down. I've been trying to do that sometimes while driving. But I flip on the radio instead. A traffic reporter is zooming through her news: "The usual delays on the outbound Edens, a gaper's block on the inbound caused by a fender bender. On the Kennedy, everything's backed up bumper to bumper." I chew my french fries like a gerbil.

At the toll booth I make for the automatic lanes, sliding across several lanes of traffic while juggling a dripping burger and an orange juice (my nod to healthy eating). *At least I've got correct change. That will save some time.*

The gate lifts and I'm off again, straining to get the inside track, as far forward as possible. I'm ahead of the other car by a hood, then a full length. I pull in, headlights looming close in my mirror, and I race towards my destination, whipping the car to a lather.

So it continues: from counseling to soccer to home, always late, always trying to catch up, but still hoping to fit in just one more activity.

No wonder I need counseling! I cringe to even think about it. This is not the way I'd like to picture myself: a member of Speedsters Anonymous. But I dare to confess because I know there are others out there, on the highways or standing in the express lane at the grocery store, feeling just as frustrated as I do.

On two occasions now, I have asked groups of U.S. Christians—over sixty people in all—to list what held them back the most spiritually. The overwhelming majority said, "I'm too busy." If they are anything like me, they have gone whole days, maybe weeks, without thinking about God—not because they didn't want to, but because they just didn't have time! That's reality for anyone living in a technologically advanced society.

Too Busy to Live?

At a one-day retreat a year ago, the spiritual director challenged us all morning to examine our sense of time. I almost left at lunch, believe it or not, because I felt an urgent need to steal back home and work on an article. Fortunately I stayed.

He asked, "When someone greets you and says, 'How's it going?' what's your typical answer?"

I knew the answer instantly, almost as if someone had shouted it out: "Busy!"

I'm always telling people I'm busy. They expect it. That's the right thing to say—the productive thing. And they always reply the way they should: "You too?" Almost as if they are pleasantly surprised: "Isn't that great: we're all in this together."

It used to be that the stock answer to "How are you?" was "Fine." Now it's "Busy." What does that mean?

It can't be good.

Brother Jolley, the leader of our retreat, insisted, "Being busy has become a way of protecting ourselves against the voice that says, 'Are you seeking my face?' " As he spoke, I examined my own life, and I had to admit he was right. Busyness insulates me from the deeper truths of life, until, of course, the busyness itself becomes unbearable.

Not so long ago, I read about an author who found his life so unbearable that he began to plan ways to commit suicide. In a desperate bid to save himself, he committed himself to a psychiatric hospital. Surprisingly, after several weeks there he returned to his family a new person. Was it the therapy that helped him? Was it the medication? No. He insisted that he had just needed the time alone. He had become so trapped in the rush of modern life that he just needed time away from it, to recover his perspective.

Like him, I have sometimes felt trapped in the rush of time. For example, the day I returned to my apartment after a weekend spiritual retreat. I stood outside in the hall, and I could hear my roommate singing with the radio inside, and I could hear all the cars swooshing by on the highway below, and there was a TV voice in the next apartment, and somewhere else the deep bass of another radio. And I felt physically assaulted by it all. Attacked!

For three days I had observed silence except at mealtimes and during worship. I had stayed in an incredibly quiet room at an abbey lost in the middle of miles of Missouri pastureland, where the only sounds were the wind and the distant chirping of birds and the occasional clang of bells. Out there, without realizing, I had been purged of my need to be pumped up, full of noise and activity. I had been detoxed.

Reservations Required

Old habits are hard to break. That's why I had to leave my environment completely to even realize what it was like. It takes that kind of radical shift to start breaking the busy habit.

In Korea, where the church has experienced such amazing growth and where people live so crowded together and busy, there is a whole mountain reserved for private retreats. People go for days, and they sit in little cavelike cells meditating and praying. This is not some sort of self-inflicted torture. It's a privilege to them. They enjoy it. It's hard to get a reservation, even months in advance.

Unless we, too, reserve time and space, how can we expect to be with God? We will always be too distracted.

Jesus certainly knew the need to reserve time with God, so he had a habit of suddenly disappearing, going away to be alone with God, often in the out-of-doors. He began his public ministry with forty days alone in the wilderness, away from all distractions (Mt 4:1-11). After miraculously feeding five thousand people with a few loaves and fish, he sent the disciples on ahead and retreated into the mountains alone to pray (Mt 14:13-24). Later, when he was transfigured by God—literally pointed out and named as God's Son—he was once again on retreat, at the top of a mountain with three chosen disciples (Mt 17:1-2). And then, after returning triumphantly to Jerusalem, he retreated one last time, to prepare himself for his painful end, alone with God in the garden of Gethsemane (Mt 26:36-45).

Jesus obviously knew the need to step out of his busyness. But the only way I personally can take time to be quiet is if I am convinced that such "unused" time is good time, *real* time. I am getting there, slowly. To really enjoy such quiet I sometimes have to forcibly remind myself that it is good for me. It helps to remember the quiet moments in my past.

A Moment of Eternity

One of the best moments of my childhood was one of the quietest. This simple moment has stayed with me over the years, ever brilliant, ever full of happiness.

School was out for the summer in our small town, Troy, Kansas, and I decided to go fishing. For some reason no one else could go, so I pedaled to the little manmade lake on the edge of town, riding my gold banana-seat bike, tackle box in one hand, pole poking out from the other hand like a thin lance.

When I got to the lake, I was the only one there. It was a very still and hot afternoon, and I'm not sure I even found the energy to watch my bobber. Instead, I got down on my hands and knees next to the water's edge, then lay down flat on my stomach, where the grass was still green, and looked into the lake. I stared down into a microcosmic world of water and weed and bluegill life, and it was as if God said, "Here is a gift, just for you." Gently, two lazy minnows wandered out of their submarine forest and into an open glade. They flitted back under a canopy of green, chasing each other. Then they came back and rested in front of me, softly pulsing with life.

It's almost impossible to explain, but for a while that summer day, as I watched those tiny fish, I left our temporal reality, escaped time altogether. God let me out!

It was as if I became a fish, and there I rested too, in the swaying water. I drifted where it took me. I relaxed so totally that I could hear the blood drumming softly in my ears. Could feel the current grow cool as I slid into the shade, grow warm again as I broke into the sun. Could see the glistening scales of my sides as I wriggled through the water, shimmering, shining, weightless, smooth as mercury, streaking the water with light.

That moment of existence, so unintentional, so silent, seems closer to eternity than most of the moments since, even those that have been filled with unusual activity and rich thought. It convinced me that life at its best has more to do with what is happening in us than outside. And that meditating on God's creation, which is a form of praying or worship, is always worthwhile.

I've had plenty of stimulation in my life, but the best moments were the simplest. So when taking time to be quiet seems to be a sacrifice, I have to remind myself that in reality it is just the opposite. For what I am yearning after is not more activity; it is rest. Even though everyone around me is shouting, "Do more, do more, or you will regret it!" I do not really want to do more. I want to *be* more. I want to *be* enough to hear the wind in the grass, to see the slow movement of the shadows as the sun trails across the sky, to feel the gentle touch of a friend, to hear the exquisite whisper of God, telling me something special that he has been waiting and waiting and waiting to say.

That is what I really want and need. How about you?

Eleven

Sunday Getaway

RETREATS ARE ONE WAY TO RADICALLY BREAK FROM our routine and find time with God. When we feel busiest we need them most. But I find I need a day that is regularly my retreat—my sabbath. With all the activity that spills into Sunday, I have almost no concept of sabbath, so I've had to start all over.

The change began one Sunday when I forgot it was Sunday! In just three weeks I had been to four countries: India, Bangladesh, Nepal and Switzerland. I had been busy every day except two, meeting with dozens of people, leading sessions at one workshop after another. Some days, I had led meetings for ten or twelve hours straight. No wonder as I made my way home I fell sick. And yet as I lay on my bed at the Glockenhof hotel in Zurich, I was enraged. I hate being slowed down!

It had started as a cold. Then, as I flew from Kathmandu to Delhi, the cold gurgled into my ears, blocking them so badly I feared I would burst an eardrum. When I got off the plane, I pounded my forehead, trying to dislodge the pressure. I paced back and forth in my hotel room, agonizing over whether to cancel the next day's flight.

If I stayed, maybe I could make headway on my trip report. I had already put it off too long. But would I be able to concentrate? And what use was it just lying around?

I called the hotel doctor, a nervous Indian with a biscuit tin full of sample medicines. He looked in my ears with a flashlight and said, "Ideally you shouldn't fly, but . . ." That "but" was enough. I took a string of decongestants, plugged my ears with foam, forced myself onto the plane and flew to Zurich. On the way I mustered just enough energy to start filling out my expense report.

In Zurich I still wasn't sure whether to continue the journey, so after I checked in at my hotel, I asked for a doctor. It was a Saturday, and the only doctor available was at the emergency room. I waited my turn, watching an old man with his nostrils distended by bloody cotton. I thought, *Look at him; you can't be that bad off.* Once again came the advice, "Of course, ideally you shouldn't fly, but . . ." And once again, that was enough. If it was at all possible, I was determined to push on. There was so much still to do.

The next morning, before checking out, I had finished only a few bites of breakfast when I had an overpowering need to find a restroom. I barely made it to my room before exploding, then lay down on the bed frustrated. *Now what?*

There may be nothing more torturous—at least for me—than being ill and alone in a strange country. Aside from the fact that it's painful and worrisome, nothing gets done. Without energy, I just lie there feeling useless.

I decided to read my Bible. Maybe I could find comfort there. I had been reading in Hebrews, so I opened to chapter four. These were the first words: "Therefore, since the promise of entering his rest still stands, let us be careful that none of you be found to have fallen short of it" (Heb 4:1).

Uh-oh!

I kept reading: "It still remains that some will enter that rest, and those who formerly had the gospel preached to them did not go in, because of their disobedience. Therefore God again set a certain day, calling it Today" (vv. 6-7).

At about that moment I realized, "This is Sunday!" With all my efforts to keep moving I had completely forgotten Sunday. The sabbath. The day of rest.

"There remains, then, a Sabbath-rest for the people of God; for anyone who enters God's rest also rests from his own work, just as God did from his. Let us, therefore, make every effort to enter that rest" (vv. 9-11).

I called the hotel manager and asked if I could keep my room for another day. He said yes. I called Swiss Air and asked if there were any seats available the next day. They said yes. I had no excuses left, so I canceled my flight.

Was that day the gentle, restful day that I hoped it would be? *No!* I tottered back and forth to the toilet, my body convulsed in an attempt to rid itself of whatever had invaded over the night. I became so dehydrated I couldn't spit. But the next day, as I eased into a seat on the plane, I thanked God for keeping me in Zurich. I would have been miserable wobbling up and down the aisle of the plane for ten hours straight. More important, I had been forced to recognize my need for rest. God was telling me to slow down, and to do it regularly.

And on the Seventh Day . . .

I remember trying once to describe for a Jewish editor at a publishing conference in New York the ways in which I struggle to stay alive spiritually. He nodded cautiously, not wanting to identify with me too much until he knew where I was going. But when I began to talk about the modern view of time, he blurted out: "That's the most important factor for me. To find time. There are other things that Judaism has given to the world, but nothing as important as the sabbath. A whole day set aside to be quiet and aware."

The traditional Jewish sabbath, the sabbath as Jesus knew it, begins at sunset on Friday evening and lats until sunset on Saturday.

During that time no one does any work. And the focus is to draw closer to God.

Try it sometime. You will be amazed how much fun it is—to not do anything, to just be. At family reunions, our family has celebrated our own version of the Jewish sabbath several times, actually putting a sign across the driveway:

> WE ARE ENJOYING A SABBATH REST
> UNTIL SUNSET TOMORROW.
> PLEASE CHECK BACK WITH US THEN.

We unplug the phones and retreat into the house, where we spend the next twenty-four hours talking and eating and resting and quietly meditating or worshiping. We begin by lighting the sabbath candles, one for creation and one for redemption. Then during dinner, our father places his hands on the heads of each of us children to give us a blessing. And indeed we are blessed—blessed by the quiet rest that we find that night and the day that follows.

Give Me That Old-Time Religion

In most affluent societies, we have moved so far away from the biblical sabbath that it is unrecognizable. I suspect Jesus' sabbath was much more like what I have experienced among Christians in traditional societies like Ethiopia.

In Bulki, Ethiopia, high in the mountains, a church service takes four to six hours. I remember our family waking early and hiking several miles to visit one of those country churches. The clouds were still lifting off the mountains, so sometimes we were in them and sometimes we weren't. When they lifted, we could see into the valley miles away, where other people were threading toward the same church in their bright white shammas.

That day, we passed through groves of dripping banana trees, leaping from stone to stone across rivers surging with rain water and red silt, before we arrived at last at a big thatched church. The service, which began around 9:00, didn't end till 1:00 or 2:00. We sat on split logs, listening to a choir, then another group of singers, and another. There were testimonies and solos and sermons—not one or two, but three. And for a full hour, we all got down on our hands and knees and pressed our faces against the clay floor to pray.

It wasn't easy for my younger brother and me, not knowing enough Amharic to follow along. Several times Mom sneaked us cookies just to keep us quiet. But for those Christians, it was obviously a pleasure to give that time to God. They were glad just to be together. They were glad to stop the routine activity of the week—the plowing and threshing and cooking and incessant hard work of survival—and just be together with God.

We had come a long way to be at rest with them. Our mountaintop home in Bulki was accessible only by air or by foot. Due to the condition of the roads, we usually came by air. We dropped in out of the sky in a little one-engine Cessna owned by the mission.

The flight down from Addis to Bulki carried us hundreds of miles into the rugged ranges of southern Ethiopia, where roads end, surrendering to threadlike paths that lead from one thatch tukel to the next. As we flew over, in between the huts we would see an occasional steep field with a farmer plodding behind oxen, plowing sideways across the mountain. And there were rivers in the valleys, digging ever-deeper ravines or spilling majestically off the crest of a cliff into the forest. But that was the only movement.

Then, to land at Bulki, the pilot had to fly straight at the mountain, swooping upward onto an uphill strip of grass only two hundred yards long. He would keep the engine racing to the top of the incline, so that we wouldn't have to push the plane. After we got off, he would spin around to face down the mountain for takeoff.

The first time I watched the plane leave, fading into a tiny white humming spot in the distance, I felt like a time traveler who had dropped out of another era. Two hours earlier, back in Addis, I had been surrounded by the concrete and iron bustle of the twentieth century. Suddenly, I had shifted to the medieval period, or further back, to the first century A.D. Time itself had changed. It didn't run the same way anymore.

Too Much Sabbath?

It was out there, where the drama of the New Testament church was still happening, that I discovered the true meaning of the sabbath. One Saturday, when we were expecting the missionary pilot to arrive to fly our family back to Addis Ababa so my younger brother and I could return to boarding school, the pilot radioed. He had put down at a station south of us and had to stay the night. He said that, as usual, he didn't plan to fly on a Sunday, but there was a slight chance he would come through if he was told to get the plane back to Addis. It wasn't likely, though.

Dad wanted to visit a church in the valley the next morning; that meant two hours of hiking. I had begun to adjust to the slower pace of this mountain area, so I agreed to go along. Mom and Nat slept in. We would try to be back by about two o'clock, just in case a flight *did* come.

Down we went, out of the lush, cloud-covered slopes into the dry, brown savannah grass below. There was the church, the congregation drifting in from trails in all directions. It was Communion Sunday, and that meant an even longer service than usual, but I don't remember being restless this time. I enjoyed the Communion. Quietly, the people passed the little bits of *injera,* a soft pancakelike bread. Then came honey water in tiny glasses, the Ethiopian version of wine. I drank it, and it filled me with warmth. I was at peace.

When the service was over, the elders begged us to stay for lunch. We knew that would take us past the deadline for our possible flight, but the sheer affection and graciousness that they showed made it impossible to say no (not to mention the sharp aroma of *injera ba wat* seeping out of the house nearby). We took our turns having warm water poured over our hands out of a clay pot and shaking our hands back and forth to dry. Then we ate to our hearts' content.

The meal, as could be expected, was delicious. There was *doro wat*, a thick, burning stew rich with chicken meat and eggs. And there was more than enough of the pliable sourdough *injera*. We all dipped into the same big round platter, laughing with satisfaction. Occasionally I had a nagging sense of the passing of time: *Maybe we shouldn't have stayed.* But there was such pleasure just being together with these fellow Christians, even despite the language barrier, that I dismissed my worries.

The sabbath continued. Until I heard it—an engine, way off in the distance, but growing louder.

"Dad, do you hear that?"

"What?"

"A plane."

"No. I don't hear anything."

I knew why he didn't hear it. He had terrible hearing. But I also knew that he didn't want to hear it. And in a way, I didn't either.

When we left the church and started back up the mountain, I pushed us to keep moving. "I'm sure I heard a plane."

"They never fly on Sundays. It's a policy."

"Yeah, but I heard something, and they said they *might* come."

We were only a half-mile away when I heard the engine again. This time very loud. "Now do you hear it?"

We began to run. And just then the Cessna came arching around the mountain. It passed right over us. Both of us shouted and waved our arms, but it didn't slow or turn. It just shot on down the valley, fixed on its schedule, operating on a time that we had forgotten about, that didn't seem possible on the sabbath.

When we got to the house, there was a note on the door. "We've gone on. Didn't know what to do. Plane will be back in two days. Key's above the door. Love, Mom."

I was angry. I shouted and banged on the door. "We shouldn't have stayed down there so long. It messed everything up." The fact was that I felt scared. I think I felt how precarious was the link between this world and the one that Mom and Nat had disappeared into. I secretly feared that we had been left in this forgotten world while they went forward into the racing future. The winged time machine had snatched them North, back to modernity. And I felt cut off in the slower South.

As it turned out, those were two of the most enjoyable days Dad and I have ever had together—quiet, contemplative, friendly. I remember spending hours learning how to cook cornbread. The two of us played chess by candlelight, late into the night, then talked even later. We could have stayed there longer, in that extended sabbath. It was hard to leave in the end.

Sabbath Is an Attitude

If I want to transform Sunday back into the sabbath, I need to learn an attitude first. I need to learn how *to be*, not *to do.* Up in the mountains of Ethiopia I was forced to let go of the need to do things, to keep moving. That's why I enjoyed the time so much. But that's tough here in the fast North, the progressive North. How can we make it happen?

When I was in junior high in a small town in Kansas, the people there used to return in groups after church to their homes, where a pot roast was bubbling and potatoes were baked and waiting. And these little groups sat for hours eating and talking. If they felt like it, they took naps. They woke whenever their bodies told them they were rested. The stores were closed. There were no Little League games. Everyone in town simply agreed to rest. And though we kids might go outside and play basketball in the driveway or ride bikes lazily down the brick-paved streets, even that was a form of rest. Nothing was planned or urgent.

Now, in most communities, the Quik Shops have invaded, and Little League is only one of many Sunday programs. Other countries around the world are following the same pattern. So to recover Sunday as the sabbath will require going against the grain. It will mean doing something unusual, perhaps even odd from the perspective of others. It will mean giving up "doing."

It may seem impossible to make Sunday into a true Sabbath; many of us are so active in the church that we never really rest or find quiet on Sunday. Maybe we need to find another day which we can set aside to rest and to speak to God. For Cathy, who is a minister, Friday is the sabbath. That is the day when she receives instead of giving. It is her day of being, not doing. She naps. She doesn't answer the phone. She takes voice lessons, and gets her hair done, and walks. She writes letters to friends. Prays. Dreams.

If nothing else, we need to turn smaller chunks of time into short sabbaths. Since creation, people have been waking early and spending time with God. They have been stopping just long enough to pray before meals, or at bedtime. These aren't out-of-date traditions. Throughout history people have chosen to stop their routine activity at these regular times. It's a way to quit hurtling through life—to catch their breath spiritually.

One way or the other, we need to build the sabbath back into our busy schedules, breaking the stranglehold of activity. This will do more to restore our inner peace and to improve our relationship with God than almost anything else.

God will meet us, if only we will get away to be with him.

Twelve

Creativity Uncaged

ONE NIGHT MY BROTHER NAT AND HIS WIFE, MARCIA, SET-tled in to watch TV, lying on their bed with a stash of junk food. But the TV wouldn't tune in. Static danced back and forth across the screen and the sound faded whenever they stood back.

They tried everything—shifting the TV, attaching a coat hanger to the antenna, then tinfoil—but as the evening wore on, they became more and more frustrated. They began to wonder why the TV was so important in the first place. Why did they have such a compulsion to sit there, ignoring each other even though they were newly married? Why couldn't they just turn the stupid thing off? They became overcome with self-loathing, almost to the point of sickness . . . until suddenly the screen went white and the whiteness compressed into a tiny dot.

Nat, who can be wonderfully straightforward, made up his mind at that instant: the TV had to go. Not only did it have to go, but it had to be destroyed. They drove to a deserted gravel road, tied the TV behind their pickup and dragged it two miles.

In case you ever decide to do the same, you should know that a TV isn't easily destroyed. The screen remained intact. Worried that this resistant invader might return to haunt them (or some other innocent soul), Nat and Marcia hoisted the metal monster into the air several times, letting it crash onto the road. At last, the screen cracked!

They were nearly satisfied, but as one last step they returned to town and hung the battered TV from a tree at the university, with a sign under it: "Stop the closing of the American mind!"

You have probably already heard warnings about the terrible evils of TV. But what if that is not the real problem?

I think Nat and Marcia know, as well as I do, that when we can't unshackle ourselves from a TV, the TV isn't the problem. For me, the real problem lies deeper, in my soul, where I am hungering for something.

Actually, for three years Cathy and I didn't have a TV. That took care of my urge to watch at home. But when I traveled to other countries through my work, I still found the pull of the TV almost irresistible, especially when I stayed in hotels alone, worn out from travel and work. To my consternation, just when I knew that I needed rest, or exercise, or something healthy, the TV seemed to reach out and handcuff me to my easy chair, keeping me there for four to six hours. It didn't matter that all I had to watch was world news in Swahili, or "Columbo" in German; still I sat there, trying to fill the empty hole in my soul. It was like eating while constantly craving more food.

I use addiction imagery intentionally. The reason I watch TV when there's nothing of significance to watch is that I am exhausted or lonely and I am trying to escape those realities. TV is my drug.

TV, if we let it, can remove us from life completely. What appears in that magical box is often something I could see directly and actively. MTV gives me a rock concert at a distance. A televised ball game gives me the actual event from hundreds of miles away. A TV film offers the movie without my traveling to the theater.

But we should not look at TV as a separate entity; it is integrally connected to all that other entertainment. And we want entertainment. In my case, I know I am looking for need-fulfillment in the entertainment itself, not just in TV. I will struggle, to varying degrees, with all my attempts to be entertained, even if I do get in the car and drive closer to the action. Almost anyone from a fast-paced entertainment culture will struggle with this same overwhelming need to be entertained.

Relaxation Is Such Work!

So why is entertainment, not just TV, so important in many modern affluent societies?

One reason is that we have a desperate need to *relax*. We try to escape into entertainment because we are too busy. Then, ironically, that entertainment only swallows up more of our time, making us feel busier, less productive. I can sit right up against the screen for an hour, my hand on the dial, trying the whole time to find some elusive ideal program. And I can waste time the same way, on a grander scale, as I switch the options for "fun" things to do on a weekend, whether that means going to a concert or a dance performance or a Chicago Bulls basketball game. I'm amazed how compulsive I can be about getting entertained. And how empty I can feel after failing to find just the right event.

True, certain performers come along at critical junctures in my life, meeting me right where I am, like the folk musician who sang to me of my lost childhood, reminding me of the importance of getting out of my brick and glass and pavement world and playing in the woods and really looking at the trees, the bark, the mottled light on the leaf-strewn ground, the swaying limbs above. That folk singer helped me to get in touch with myself. He inspired me to live more fully.

Or I think of the film *Awakenings*—how I wept as I watched Robert de Niro struggling not to fall back into a catatonic state after miraculously awakening from a coma. And how it hurt to recognize my own tendency to live locked inside myself, like the caged panther de Niro read about in a Rilke poem, pacing back and forth and back and forth behind the bars, wanting to get out, to be fully what it was meant to be.

Such performances help us discover ourselves. But you be the judge: Are you relaxed after the entertainment you choose? Do you feel filled with peace? Closer to yourself and God?

On the contrary, I find that the average movie or rock concert or professional sporting event leaves me filled with raucous noise and stimulation. I have fun. It's a sort of high. But the event removes me from myself, rather than bringing me into touch. I stumble out of the theater and am shocked by the cold rain, a wet slap of reality. It's almost as if I forgot I had a body. Or I come home from the concert with ringing ears and can't find the concentration to do anything.

I like entertainment. But how do I put it in proper perspective?

Professionals Not Needed

One way we can help ourselves is to recover the art of entertaining ourselves. Before TV, families were much more inclined to retire into "the parlor," where they would sing together or play games or listen to someone read. Today, in slower-paced societies, entertainment is still simple and participatory. And it is delightful.

Once, in India, a Christian friend invited me to his home to meet his wife and four children. After a rich meal—better than any I had eaten at Indian restaurants—Mohan announced that his two daughters had a dance to perform. They disappeared, giggling, and came back wearing beautiful white embroidered blouses and loose white pants with tight ankles. Their wrists jangled with a dozen small bracelets.

The two girls struck an elegant pose, facing each other with arms bent and hands lifted in mirrorlike imitation. When the music began, they spun slowly, lifting their feet in unison and gently stomping them down. They swayed toward each other and apart, their poised motions always in duplicate. As I watched, seeing the joy flashing in their eyes, I was filled with contentment. It was a delight to meditate on their lithe youthfulness, their charm, their skill. And I could see that they were delighted to receive this attention. The mother of the girls was happy too, because she had cooked a triumph of a meal, and we had let her know how good it was.

I remember another family dinner, this time in Tanzania, where our host said that his children wanted to sing. "By all means," we said. The children lined up by height, like a miniature choir, and began. Their high, tremulous voices harmonized as only African voices can, using notes that don't seem to exist on the Western musical scale. And the Swahili language, so full of open vowels, spilled off their lips warm and sweet as honey. Again, I was filled with contentment. They ministered to me with this gift. And I ministered to them by receiving the gift.

How are these "events" different from the big events that I gravitate toward here at home?

For starters, they don't separate people. Rather than forcing the audience into distant seats to focus on a few unreachable professionals, these little performances encourage everyone in the room to see themselves as equally gifted and worthwhile. We are not cut off by performing; we are not lost in a faceless crowd of viewers; we are found. And all that without the long drive, the packed parking lot, the ticket-booth hubbub that go with professional performances. Even better, all that without the acid indigestion and emptiness that come when we watch TV alone and exhausted, so far away from real life that we might as well be sitting on the moon.

Stage Fright?

So why don't we do more of this simple home entertainment?

In my case, I think it's both fear and fatigue. I am afraid to experiment because it would seem amateur—because it would force people to be uncomfortably personal. What's more, I am too tired to be creative when I want to be—too busy and distracted, often because I have been running around trying to get entertained. So I opt to sit back passively and watch someone else be creative.

It makes me mad just to think about it. I could find both beauty and meaning in my own community.

What delight I have experienced the few times friends were brave enough to share with me the gifts they have. I think, for example, of Jack, a gruff retired engineer. He had hinted to Cathy and me that his hobby was music. He seemed to go to the opera constantly, taking his wife along. We could picture her there, but we weren't so sure about Jack. With his seemingly restless personality, we didn't expect such a love for music. But one night we coaxed him into playing a few numbers on the piano, and something amazing happened.

As his fingers glided across the keys, gently interpreting Schubert, then pounded their way through Beethoven, I watched Jack's rough, weathered face. It was the same face I had seen a hundred times at our church, all the more ruddy because of his shock of white hair, and yet suddenly it was a different face. He had become real for me. As he poured himself into that piano, I believe God showed him to me as he truly was. And what a gift!

Because Cathy and I enjoy such moments of creative sharing, we have developed a type of party that we like to throw. The only prerequisite is that everyone bring something to share: a poem, a children's story, a song, a bit of handcraft. Just something.

Once we held such a party on a St. Patrick's Day, to celebrate Cathy's heritage. The mix was a delight. There was an Irish legend about Countess Cathleen, who was so generous and loving that she was willing to sell her soul to the devil so that her people would be freed from famine. There were several simple Irish blessings and a tape of Irish humor. And to finish the evening, we lit a candle and let one friend read the powerful prayer "Patrick's Breastplate." Another couple sang the same prayer as a hymn.

We have even done the same thing for the whole church, organizing a "Creativity Night" and inviting everyone to share their talent, whether it took the form of a model railroad, a poem, a hand-knitted sweater or a special dessert. Over and over I heard it that night as I walked around the room: "I had no idea we had so much talent right in our own church. It's wonderful!"

Encouragement Always Helps

But someone needs to be the "encourager," if creativity is to occur. There are too many reasons to put it off—too many excuses.

A friend who is an inner-city teacher argues with me. "I think you have got to realize that the TV teaches things kids couldn't learn otherwise." She thinks people need professional entertainment, even if only on television. "The kids I work with are caught in little worlds—the school, their little apartment, the park, that's it. They need the TV. It shows them what's out there. It's their only connection."

I agree. For many people, TV is a vital link with a larger society which would pass them by otherwise. It gives them entertainment they can afford—and everyone needs entertainment. It also educates, bringing the outside world into the home so they can reflect on it. TV gives us all a collective understanding about life.

But I lament what holds people in front of the TV long past the time needed for learning something new or taking a break—what holds them there when they could be exploring their own talents or investing them for the future. I lament the desperate need to escape into entertainment.

Those inner-city kids choose to escape, as my friend herself admits, because most of them simply don't believe they are creative enough to entertain themselves or to be productive. And there aren't enough caring people like that teacher, constantly encouraging kids to express themselves, building their confidence. That's why they don't discover their talents.

My friend is also right when she points out that it's easy for us to take for granted the support we had when growing up. From the day I was born, unlike many children, I was encouraged to be creative. I had that kind of family. A virtual cheering squad. And I had that kind of teachers. Experimenting (no matter how outlandish the results) was okay.

I look back now and laugh, thinking of some of the things I was allowed to create as a child. But I learned from each project. When I was eleven, for instance, I built a medieval catapult.

That's right, a catapult!

It all started when my grandfather noticed my interest in a book in his eclectic basement library titled *Weapons: A Pictorial History.* He gave it to me. But instead of just reading it, I tried to create the objects etched there. I forged myself a sword of plywood and tinfoil, and I armored myself with plastic milk cartons. Then I made the mistake of looking in a mirror.

Suddenly I decided to shoot for something more substantial, more authentic. Nothing else would do. It had to be a medieval catapult.

I wanted lumber, nails, hinges, power tools. If ever my parents had a right to say, "No, this will not work—we don't pay for tomfoolery," this was the time. Instead, they actually helped me build—they provided the materials I needed. To my surprise I found a stack of two-by-fours in the garage, with a box of nails on top. No power tools. I would just have to use old-fashioned muscle power. But everything I really needed was there.

The central force of the medieval catapult is a huge rock weight which drops down, making the other end of a beam flip into the air, flinging a small boulder with intent to destroy. This approach seemed unlikely to me at the time, so I drew up plans for something that looked like a catapult but acted like a slingshot—a sort of "catasling."

I remember that the crowning glory of this updated machine was a five-foot tube of surgical rubber the diameter of a garden hose. Dad, a doctor, brought it home from the surgical supply house, and I raced all over the house snapping it gleefully at my brothers.

Finally the moment of unveiling arrived. I raised the garage door and slid the catasling out into the walled driveway. The whole family stood above, looking down expectantly, like a full-capacity stadium crowd.

Since I had created a lethal weapon and it faced a widow's house across the street, I was told to shift it. That way the projectile would hurtle into her yard or the alley beyond, rather than putting a hole in her roof.

I pulled back the rubber tubing with a pulley I'd rigged. I dropped a heavy rock into the wooden firing bucket. And then, feeling like Gregory Peck in *The Guns of Navarone,* I released the drawstring.

The little bucket shot forward, up the firing chute, and clapped to a stop. The rock sailed on—ten, twelve, a full fifteen feet. Plop. It plummeted undramatically onto the driveway.

For a moment I reflected on the fact that I could probably have thrown the rock as far and with much less effort. Then I bowed to my clapping (and smiling) fans and explained that I was still perfecting the catasling; I would need a little more time.

It's been twenty years and I still haven't perfected it. But what matters to me is not that I failed to shoot the rock over the widow's house, only that I succeeded in getting as far as I did. Because my parents respected my interests and aspirations, they let me explore, even helped me explore. They gave me an alternative to the narrower world of TV and professional entertainment. And so they helped me break the grip of entertainment.

Don't Bury Those Talents

The fact is that all creative endeavors, no matter how odd they may seem to others, are an expression of our talents, and without talents we wither. Even if our creativity is never shown to others, it is a blessing.

A good friend of ours is a painter. She spends hours every day in her studio painting. If she goes too long without painting she begins to act hyperactive—to lose track of where she is or what she is doing. Selling her work, or having it seen by others, is secondary. She just enjoys creating. She says that's because her painting, like prayer, puts her in a meditative state. It slows life and lets her react to it. It lets her work her feelings out where she can see them—on the canvas.

Certainly writing does the same for me. If I go too long without writing, I begin to feel hopelessly rushed—out of control. But at such times, almost any creativity seems to relieve the pressure. For instance, I also like to sculpt. In fact, I may find sculpting even more relaxing and enjoyable than writing, because I don't have to do it on a professional level. I'm very much an amateur. When I take a block of limestone, two hundred pounds heavy, and begin to bash away at it, uncovering the form inside, I simply get pleasure out of the process. I'm glad the stone resists. I'm glad my arms ache. I feel very alive. And as much as I love sitting in an audience to watch someone else perform, this hard work seems twice as refreshing as a "show."

It makes sense, doesn't it? If we are made in God's image and God is a Creator, then we are made to create. The joy we feel in creating is the joy of being fully ourselves.

No excuses. Even though we may not all be great artists, I am convinced that somewhere each of us has a special gift, some creative practice: doing woodwork, pottery, crocheting, poetry, cooking, gardening, playing the ukelele, you name it.

One woman writes a letter every day. That's a beautiful expression of who she is—a thoughtful, intentionally loving person. And like her, each of us is a unique member of Christ's body, with our own unique ways of ministering to others.

I have always been struck by the pun that is built into Christ's parable about the rich man's "talents." A rich man goes away, entrusting his coins, or talents, to three servants. Two invest their talents so that they are multiplied. They risk taking these talents out into the open, into public places. The third servant, afraid, perhaps tired or lonely, buries his talent in the hope that at least he won't lose it while the master is away. To his surprise, the master returns, takes that one talent away and gives it to the other servants, then banishes this passive pessimist, telling him that he has wasted what was given to him (Mt 25:14-30).

In the First World, we are all tired. We need rest. We will be tempted to bury our talents in the soft recesses of the living-room couch, protecting them while we look to televised performers for entertainment. We think we will find safety and rest there, but ironically we lose both, and life with it. We fall back into the comfort trap.

Creativity, by contrast, is life-giving. When we are being creative—like God—we draw near to God. We become more meditative, more conscious of reality, of God himself. We *live* instead of just surviving.

Thirteen

Back to Nature

PEOPLE TALK ABOUT HATING THEIR BODIES. THEY CAN'T stand being so fat or skinny, so tall or short, having straight hair or curly, having no hair at all. They lament ample bottoms or grieve over flat ones. In an attempt to exercise some control over it all, they lift weights, dye their hair, suck fat out of their hips, get breast implants, grow a beard, buy a girdle, get shoes with heels, walk with a slouch, avoid smiling too widely.

I used to laugh: *Why all this fuss? God gives you what he gives.*

As for my body, it has provided a lot of pleasure. It has carried me out into the muffled silence of snowfall, tingling with cold. It has filled me with satisfaction as I've eaten a favorite food. It has taken me dashing out onto a wonderfully wide, green, sunlit, breezy field, to kick at a spinning ball—to delight in sheer movement.

And in those moments at home with Cathy, when we have been entirely naked, touching and being touched, my body could not be equalled for its worth. What a marvel it has been.

Perhaps I have had less to complain about than some; God has done well by me. But still, I look in the mirror: I know I'm far from perfect. Turn me sideways and I practically disappear, being all flat planes and

a few jutting outcrops: a nose, a bottom, a bit too much stomach. I'm
no movie star. But hate my body? No way!

Unless I stop to think about it more honestly.

I get sick a lot. Sinusitis. When a week has passed with a cold I
want to amputate my nose—just chop it off. I hate not being able to
wake up, to think clearly, to go out jogging. My body is nothing but
a pain.

When the cold clears up, do I feel reconciled to my body? I ought
to, but often I don't. I *still* find it frustrating to wake so slowly. I *still*
fight against going to bed, indignant that I can't run nonstop, twenty-
four hours a day. And when I'm just a little too slow kicking the
soccer ball—when I see the goal fill up with players before I can
react—I don't like my body at all. It's stupid. It gets in the way.

As for my sexuality (that hot southern part of me, so full of unpredictable weather), I enjoy my visits there, but sometimes I come back
completely frustrated. Why do my eyes wander so much? Why do my
glands surge? Why don't I have more control over this stirring, never-
satisfied part of me?

Do I hate my body? Yes, like others, sometimes I do. Some days we
just don't get along.

I shouldn't be so surprised. How can I be reconciled to my body
when I live as if it didn't exist? For that's what I've been doing much
of my life, just as I have learned to do with all of creation.

Getting Our Bodies Back

In the modern technological world it is easy to shut nature out. I turn
on the lights at night, acting as if the setting of the sun never happened, as if all the stars had fallen out of the sky. I live indoors all
day, treating the fluttering leaves outside my window like a set of
plastic products from Taiwan. I eat so much packaged food that I
begin to believe eggs and milk grow in cardboard cartons, pork chops
are manufactured in Iowa, pears come in iron shells that require can
openers. And me? I'm just a spirit caught in a material world.

I am not part of nature, because I don't feel physical at all. My body is a foreign substance that I'm forced to carry around. It's as foreign to me as the chickens and cows and pigs and pear trees that produce what I eat every day.

Cloistered as I am, living in a convenience culture, I can practically deny that I even have a body! Or I can get so removed from that body that I don't know how to take care of it. Even if I am desperately shaping it at the health center, doing arm curls to build my biceps or situps to flatten my stomach, I can reach a place where I do not know or care for my body because, like all of nature, it has become foreign to me. It is like so much inert earth, needing to be shifted or flattened before the highway can go through. Nothing more than an obstacle.

So how do I recover respect for my body?

One way is by returning to nature.

When I take my body out into its natural surroundings, where it belongs, I become more connected with physical reality. Nature is not always welcoming or comfortable, but it is physically real, and it reminds me that I too am physically real. One of the unexpected bonuses of feeling so real is that I recover my sense of being a creature, and that means I recover my sense of the Creator. Suddenly God is real too.

When I think back to the moments when I have felt closest to God, the picture comes into focus slowly, but I am usually out-of-doors: on a rock in a river, at the edge of a cliff, even lying on the grass in my yard, just somewhere in nature. I find God waiting for me there, when I risk going to look for him.

Why?

Because he is expressed so clearly there. No longer is he screened by the things—necessary and convenient though they may be—which block our view: paved streets, brick buildings, giant billboards, fences, wires, rushing metal vehicles. I am thrust into the reality of his creation, which reflects him more directly than all the things that people create (even though we are indebted to him for our very capacity to create).

I characterize these moments in nature—these rare epiphanies—as gifts. It is as if I have been blind and suddenly God gives me the gift of sight, as if I have been starving and suddenly there is food. One moment, I am poor; the next, I am the wealthiest man alive. Like the psalmist I want to shout out, "O LORD, our Lord, how majestic is thy name in all the earth!" I am overcome with the same awe. "When I look at the heavens, the work of thy fingers, the moon and the stars which thou hast established; what is man that thou art mindful of him, the son of man that thou dost care for him? Yet thou hast made him little less than God, and dost crown him with glory and honor" (Ps 8:1, 3-5 New Oxford Version). Through nature I enter into worship—I reach the proper state of humility and wonder for approaching God.

God's Hidden Graces

I am walking up to the pasture behind my parents' house one wintry evening, expecting nothing, totally unprepared for the gift that is coming. It is nearly dusk, and as I climb out of the dark wooded draw onto the plateau above, the sunlight comes streaming toward me in great golden swaths, lighting up the red-tinted prairie grass so that it seems to burn. The sun is down below the clouds, and it lights up the vast hooded ceiling of the sky like burnished brass.

Suddenly the grass in front of me explodes. A covey of quail lift into the air, clapping and drumming their wings like an army of victorious angels. They gather speed as they swing in a tight circle, out over the flaming grass. Then they hurtle back past me, into the safety of the dark twiggy draw, leaving a whistling noise in their wake.

I watch where the quail disappear, then follow, hoping once again to come upon them. This time perhaps, if I am cautious, I will find them before they flee, spotting them in holy, hidden silence—still sentinels waiting for sunset and the safety of night, waiting to begin their plaintive nighttime song, bob-white, bob-white, bob-white. And so I enter the woods stealthily, each step a deliberate strategy.

As I near the area where I expect to see the quail, an unexpected movement makes me look upward. A hawk has gotten there before me. He shifts noiselessly on a branch ten feet above the ground. He cocks his head to one side, peering and listening. He cocks his head the other way, waiting and hoping. I step closer, then closer, also waiting, also hoping.

Soon I am only twenty feet away. I freeze, satisfied now to watch. I am so close I can see the eyes of the hawk, red beads ringed by black. His tail fans out in white and black bars. His chest is a smooth plume of zigzagging white and tan. After a minute, he spreads his wings, faking a takeoff. Then he stops and listens, his head cocked.

Suddenly he is in the air, diving. Only when he is inches from the ground does he open his wings, gliding across ten or fifteen feet of ground. Then he swoops up, claws empty, and turns tightly, landing back on the same branch.

Nothing moves. The shadows deepen. My breath rises in a white mist.

Again the hawk dives, this time letting his wings brush the grass, making a beating, rushing noise. And again he rises to the branch, claws empty. Nothing stirs. I stare and stare at the grass, trying to find the quail, knowing, just as the hawk knows, that they are there, also waiting, their hearts throbbing, silent like children swallowing their breath during hide-and-seek. But I can't find even one.

For five minutes, then ten, I watch the hawk hunting the phantom quail. He grows restless, less careful in his attacks. The sun sets and the woods fill with heavier and heavier shadows. Finally the hawk gives up, shooting straight down the draw toward some faraway destination. But still I don't move. Though my joints are stiffening in the chill air, I wait.

Are the quail here? And where? Or have they somehow fooled us both, moling their way through the grass and under the leaves of last fall, into some other refuge? I wait and wait, and when it seems that now it is too dark to see anything, I take a step forward, forced to abandon the search.

Thump-thump-thump-thump-thump. The quail explode out of the ground all around me. In front, to the sides, even behind. They flush out of the brush like grace, something that cannot be taken but is unexpectedly offered. And they whistle away into the night, leaving me alone.

No, not alone. Now, more than ever, I am with God, my powerful and loving Creator. And I can feel him breathing my breath, pumping my heart, absorbing the chill of the settling night. I don't want to go in, because I am closer to him than I have been in weeks or months. I am filled with thankfulness. Look what God has given me! What a gift! O LORD, our Lord, how majestic is thy name in all the earth!

Lessons Bigger Than Language

The fact is that we are ourselves a part of nature, so we have much to learn from it, much to gain. I think about a moment of discovery that I had late one afternoon, as I drove home from work, full of the distractions of day-to-day life, full of motion. I was so struck by the calmness of the rising moon that I began to write in my journal as I drove.

Right now the earth is spinning. I am moving at hundreds or thousands of miles an hour—hurtling along. At the same time I am driving. I happen to be going east—with the spin of the earth. But sometimes I drive west—like an insect trying to stay on top of a rolling log.

The moon is spinning too, though it appears to be stamped into the sky like a newly minted dime. It is not nearly as fixed as it seems, but somehow I live with the illusion that it *is* fixed, that we are fixed too, on a fixed flat surface, that the earth is as stationary as a stone bench.

Usually, I am aware that my life is spinning—sometimes out of control—but I forget that my whole universe is spinning. It makes sense, though. We are both creatures, me and the earth, me and the moon. God made us all. And probably, if I could only find a way,

I would benefit from watching how these other creatures spin—so majestically, so steadily, so utterly poised and balanced.

One thing I know: God did not make us to be still. He made us all to move, and to change. And I suspect, looking at this rising moon, that he also made us with some ideal order in mind. I think he wants us all to move gracefully—in cycles. He has seasons for us all.

I should have stopped the car and gotten out—out of that little glass-and-steel shell. I would have learned even more by being physically in touch with the world I was observing. The very reason I was so struck by nature was that I had become so detached from it.

Breaking Out of the Shell

Epiphanies can happen wherever there is even a touch of nature, even in our back yard. But unless we get out of our mechanical shells, they can't happen. In a sense, all our houses and office buildings and cars are prisons. They keep us cut off from creation . . . and from God.

I find it helpful to challenge myself with questions: "When was the last time you went camping? All right, if you can't get away for that long, what about a walk in a forest preserve, even a walk around the block? Have you been staying inside during your lunch break? Get out then."

A couple of friends and I play wiffleball during our lunch break. We look odd in button-down shirts and ties, flailing at a little plastic ball, but we come back to work refreshed—more in touch with physical reality. We come into the building a little freer than we went out.

Others choose gardening as a way to stay connected to the physical world. They insist that there is nothing quite like burying a seed and watching it become a plant (and then eating it) to remind them that they are part of creation.

Iowa folk singer Greg Brown agrees. He celebrates this wonder in a song about, of all things, his grandmother's canned food:

She cans the pickles, sweet and dill,

and the songs of the whippoorwill,
and the morning dew and the evening moon.
I really got to go down and see her soon,
'cause the canned goods that I buy at the store
ain't got the summer in them anymore.
You bet gramma, sure as you're born,
I'll take some more potatoes and a thunderstorm.[1]

When I heard him swaying his way through these lyrics, eyes closed, head swinging with yearning, I couldn't believe that a song about jars in a fruit cellar could be so moving, so absolutely compelling. But it was. That's because I was hungry for more than home-canned food. I was hungry for the life on his grandmother's farm, closer to nature, full of all the simple wonder that goes with it. When Brown got done, I agreed with the woman who shouted out, "We want to go home with you. Can we?"

We all want to go back to that world. Our bodies want to take us there. After all, they are part of it.

Who Said Nature Was Nice?

Of course, nature is not always nice. Sometimes, in fact, it is terrifying—as it was for me in 1979, when there were only one hundred miles of paved road in all of Sudan. We drove forty of those paved miles, going out of Khartoum on a trip to southern Sudan. Then the road stopped. In front of our Land Rover was an endless flat horizon, with not a building or person or animal to break its eerie sameness. And leading into it was nothing but a wide swath of tire ruts, crisscrossing through the brush.

As Dad dipped the Land Rover down onto those tracks, leaving the relative safety of the blacktop, I had to forcibly swallow a desire to shout out, "No! Let's go back." I stayed that way for hours, even though I discovered that there were old telegraph poles to use as bearings (where they hadn't been cut down for firewood).

I was filled with even more dread when we passed the first houses.

They were abandoned, with sand dunes climbing against their crumbling walls or spilling through their windows. As we went on I felt as if I were on board Columbus's ship, fearfully picturing the day we would reach the edge of the earth and the ship would be swept over, down a roaring cascade of sea water into eternal darkness.

We drove for hours under the baking sun, sweating in the hold of our tiny landlocked ship, and when we stopped to relieve ourselves, I was almost afraid to get out. I watched where I put my feet. I ducked behind a bush for a minute and came back quickly, glad to see the Land Rover was still there.

By nightfall, we still hadn't reached our destination, the little city of Renk. We had come to a huge irrigation scheme, which meant we were close. But getting through the maze of ditches and canals became increasingly difficult. Harun, the Sudanese pastor who was with us, didn't seem perturbed. He was sure we were near. But Dad couldn't see where we were going. The telegraph poles disappeared in the dark. Then the tire tracks.

My brothers and I got out and walked in front of the Land Rover to make sure we didn't drive into one of the irrigation trenches. Cut off on all sides, we finally circled, crossing our own tracks. Pastor Harun got out then and stretched, and when he had looked up at the stars, he said simply, "Renk is that way."

We had never thought to ask him, and now it was too late. Even if Renk was near, we couldn't find our way out of this trap of irrigation trenches. So we all bedded down around the Land Rover. I remember being afraid of the ground, imagining all sorts of snakes and tarantulas and what-have-you, but now I was more tired than afraid. I slept pretty well.

The next morning I was one of the first to wake, and I dared to walk a short way into the brush, going in the direction Pastor Harun had pointed. About a mile away, I came over a slight rise, and there was a building with a tin roof. All that time, we had been circling almost within earshot of Renk!

When you haven't been in nature for a while, it has an incredible ability to confuse and even terrify. Inner-city kids, when they go camping—even kids from gangs—become frightened by the noise of tree branches scraping, the call of an owl, a sudden croak from the lake. They are afraid to lose sight of a road, unlike Pastor Harun, who knew the stars like friends, recognizing them all in their proper places, neatly lined up like the telegraph poles we had been following through the desert. Pastor Harun climbed out of that Land Rover and immediately knew where he stood. He knew where he stood in relation to nature. And I think he knew better, as a result, where he stood in relation to God.

It won't do, obviously, to idolize nature and natural living, as if we should all strip and live in caves. But I am convinced that some of God's gifts will stay out of our reach until we get outside the trap of convenience and security here in the modern technological world.

Leaving our security can be frightening and confusing at first, as it was traveling across Sudan at night. But I have learned since then that if I risk going out into the natural world, eventually God meets me there, and in his arms I am safer than in my own shelters. I am more cared for.

Cared for—Body and Soul

As a teenager in Sudan, sitting in the Land Rover at the end of the paved road, I was terrified. But more recently, when I found myself once again on the edge of what we call civilization, I had a different reaction.

Cathy and I had traveled to Tanzania to visit an old friend, a missionary in a village on the edge of the Serengeti Game Park. This village, Majahida, is a long way from Chicago: fifteen hours by jet to Nairobi, an hour and a half by small plane to Lake Victoria, then five hours of bone-crushing broken roads. But the psychological distance is even greater. That came home powerfully when Cathy and I accompanied our friend Brian to a simple memorial service at the home of an old farmer whose sister had just died.

We walked on a hot dirt path, skirting piles of sweet potatoes spread out on the rocks to dry. Occasionally we had to step over a trail of ants, busily twisting their way back and forth across our path. A fig tree spread its huge branches overhead, offering refuge from the sun. It was such an impressive meeting place, all beaten flat with the feet of hundreds of people and goats and cattle, that I could see why it was considered sacred by those still adhering to the traditional religion.

When we arrived at the farmer's home, he was sitting outside with a friend playing a game that some say was the first ever played. It involved moving dark, shiny nuts across a wooden board with cuplike depressions. The board showed the wear of their endless play. The men sat on equally worn hand-carved stools. They stood as we approached, and I noticed a transistor radio sitting in the dust. In front of it were two light green batteries, waiting to be used.

The men were both older than most, but the owner of the farm was oldest. His hair was peppered, his eyes smoky with age. He was a big, portly man, and his lower teeth had a wide gap, which gave him a jovial appearance. He laughed as he talked.

When they had greeted us, holding our hands warmly, the old man fetched his best chairs for us—two bentwood chairs strapped together with tight leather. When he set them down, the leather seats thumped like drums.

All of this is what I was seeing and hearing, but it does not get at what I was feeling. As our friend Brian began the service, reading from his Swahili Bible, I was overwhelmed by the great distance we had come to sit with this old man, trying to share his grief. And I was overwhelmed by the great out-of-doors vastness around us. What a place to die—to be buried. This woman who had died, whoever she was, seemed so small to me, as I sat there in the open fields. So swallowed up and insignificant.

The farmer opened his Bible, clumsily, with thick dark fingers. He reached in his shirt pocket for a pair of ancient glasses, the lenses clouded with scratches. When he put them on he had to cock his head, using one eye more than the other, to follow the neat little print.

Here he was, so far from the rush of modernity that he could never really be part of it. The glasses themselves—such an anomaly out in this dusty, henpecked yard—were one of his few ties to what we call progress. The other ties were the transistor radio and the batteries, and his clothes.

He wore a button-down blue shirt, frayed at the neck and sleeves, with dark smudges in several spots. His polyester pants were the color of earth. On his sturdy, chapped feet he wore handmade sandals with rubber-tire soles. If I had met him on a street in Chicago, I would have classified him as homeless. But as I watched him reading his Bible, I suddenly saw him as he was: a productive citizen, a village leader, an *mzee,* as they say in Tanzania.

If I could quit classifying him from my perspective, as a visitor from the modern world, he had a natural aura of authority. When he greeted us, he did so as the owner of all the land we could see. His wife and her sister, and a child who somehow belonged here, all sat to one side, quiet. His friend, as well, took a quiet, deferential stance. This man was obviously someone to listen to, to respect, to enjoy.

Coming from my busy world of technological progress, where people have set the pace for the rest of the world, living lives that others can only dream about, at first I found myself feeling sorry for this man. He seemed so far from all the resources. Lost in the wilderness. How could he ever have an impact on the world? Yet when I thought about it more, I realized that my criteria were all wrong. *What does it matter if he is modern or not? If he is wealthy? The modern countries of this world are full of people searching for themselves. This man, at least, knows himself, and he knows God. Out here he knows what it is to be human.*

During Brian's meditation on the Scripture (a passage from Isaiah), the sun began to set. Birds settled in the little tree over our heads.

They chattered noisily. Suddenly Cathy jerked forward, flinging her hair back and forth. A baby bird dropped onto the ground. It sat there confused as we laughed. Then it lifted off and crashed into the bushes, learning to fly.

The farmer's friend began collecting the dark nuts off the playing board. It was nearly dark, and we needed to go, so we rose and circled, shaking hands again.

As we walked back to Brian's house, the sun set on one side of the path, silhouetting the earthen huts against a red sky. The moon rose, all yellow, on the other side. People called out from the shadows, wishing us well, sending us on our way with their blessings. I felt swallowed up in the darkness, yet not alone or insignificant. I felt at one with the natural world. Nature wasn't my enemy, as it sometimes seems in the orderly North. It was part of me and I part of it. I felt that to die here would be as good a place as any. And that this little gathering was as important a way to be remembered as any. It was a memorial service I will never forget.

O LORD, our Lord, how majestic is thy name in all the earth!

Fourteen

Liberty for All

USUALLY, WHEN THE PLANE LIFTS OFF, I FEEL RELEASED from more than gravity. I leave all the worries of day-to-day life down on the ground, along with the routine demands of work and the complications of relating to people. I leave time itself. Suspended 30,000 feet above normality, with the engines humming, I grow philosophical, and that leads to writing, one of my favorite pastimes.

But on a trip to Nairobi one summer, when I began to write I just felt lonely. I looked around. People were all around me, walking the aisles and talking, but it was as if they were characters in a film. They seemed that separate. My few attempts at conversation led nowhere, and I began to feel, oddly enough, as if I had been placed in solitary confinement.

It was a relief, later, to run into Vi and Jeff at the Nairobi Airport Restaurant. Both were in transit as I was, both were American, both were passionate in their views about the needs of the world.

Vi, about fifty-five, was returning to Uganda after a visit to her grown-up children in the U.S. She had lived in East Africa for twenty years, teaching biology at various schools. When I asked what had taken her there, she explained that she was Baha'i and, for lack of a better term, a missionary.

She seemed very normal for a Baha'i missionary, with her gray-blond hair and warm, weathered smile. Not like the outlandish young zealot I would have pictured! I found her easy to talk with, and it came as no surprise that she had eight children, four of whom were adopted Ugandans. She was eager to get back to them.

Jeff, a former Peace Corps worker, was younger, more cautious. He sat down at our table last, looking as if he hadn't decided whether to acknowledge us. But he had no choice. We drew him into conversation, learning that he was on his way to Zaire to reunite with his Zairian wife and to find work.

Jeff explained that there are three types of Peace Corps volunteers: those who get more than they bargained for and quit; those who stick it out, then file the experience; and those who get it in their blood and can't stay away. He didn't have to tell us which he was.

We covered a lot of territory, the three of us. And in the process God untied some knots for me, particularly about being Christian in the U.S.

Vi, who had been back to the U.S. for the first time in years, was disillusioned. "People complain so much!" she said. "And about the smallest things—like their dishwashers. In Uganda I don't have one. I don't even have running water. But they complain about water spots on the drinking glasses."

Jeff broke in, "Their standards are different, that's all. It's what they are used to."

"But I'm not used to it. Their needs are so small."

"You don't think they have needs?" he retorted. "There are people dying at home in the U.S. with no one to care. There are people who can't get a decent education."

"But the needs seem bigger here," she replied. "I mean, in Uganda everyone has a family member dying of AIDS. That's what I'm going home to do—to help a close friend die. Her husband was promiscuous and now they are both going to die, leaving four children."

I broke in then. "Actually, I think there are a lot of needs back in the U.S. But they are more difficult to deal with. That's because the needs are so complex. I mean, I'm a magazine editor, but when I think about editing material for U.S. readers, I don't know how to do it. There are so many magazines in the U.S.! People aren't looking for new ones. Their need is how to strip away all the excess—the stuff that appears in the mailbox whether or not they want it."

Jeff jumped back in. "Well, I don't think we can just dismiss a whole country. We would never say, 'Oh, forget Ethiopia. It's just too complicated to deliver relief there!' If the relief was getting siphoned off, then we would figure out a way to protect it. We would do something! The same is true for the States. Maybe we can't do much. But we shouldn't expect to be their saviors anyway."

"I don't *want* to be their savior," Vi blurted out.

I laughed. "I don't either. But I guess I agree with Jeff. In college I used to think, *As soon as I get done, I'm out of here. I'll get on the first plane back to Africa and be done with it all.* But I've changed. Personally, I feel I've got to figure out how to live in the U.S. To be honest, I think a lot of Americans come to developing countries because it's *easier.* They can measure their progress. They feel useful. I mean, I've met a lot of good missionaries, but the bad ones never realize that they are actually here to escape from their problems. They think they come to give, but really they are mostly getting."

I worried that I might have hurt Vi's feelings, but she was nodding in agreement. Jeff, on the other hand, still wasn't sure where he came down. He looked ready to do battle again, then suddenly realized it was time for his flight to Zaire.

It was hard to see our little group break up, because I felt as if God had seen my loneliness and answered an unspoken prayer. Even though these two other people were not Christians, God had brought them together with me, and I didn't like giving them up. We had become friends quickly.

As we watched Jeff walk to the elevator, Vi spoke up, "I guess I really pushed a button when I said there weren't any needs in the U.S."

"No question," I replied. "But I'll bet there's a reason. I'll bet it wasn't so long ago that Jeff himself wanted to escape the U.S. Or maybe there's something he has had to leave unresolved back in the States."

"Well, he's right. I'm probably too disillusioned. But it's hard. I'm at that age when I have to decide about the future, and to be honest I'd rather just stay in Uganda. I feel better about living with my Ugandan children than with my children in the States. I go to visit them back there, and it's true we haven't seen each other for a long time, but it just doesn't work well. You know, the mother-in-law thing. But here, I'm welcome. It doesn't matter that I'm getting old. I can still be useful."

I had to agree: It would be good for her to stay in Uganda, and good for others. *But what about me,* I found myself wondering. *Would it be good for me to stay?*

Looking for a Home

With all our differences, Vi and I had touched on a lot of common feelings. Like her, I have often wondered whether I belong in the U.S. You may understand the feeling, if you live in an affluent modern setting and you have stepped out of it briefly (or even if you haven't). Wouldn't it be nice to just get out and stay out? To go some place where life isn't so busy and complex? Where people care for each other more, and God's presence is evident?

I long for this other world, though I suspect it doesn't really exist, not until heaven. I suspect that if I were to go to Uganda, I wouldn't feel I had escaped. I might enjoy new freedoms, but I'd have to exchange them for new restraints. Vi gets sick constantly, fighting malaria, amoebic dysentery, hepatitis, worms and a host of other parasites. She is surrounded by two to four million people suffering from

AIDS. Day-to-day survival is a terrible chore there, where a teacher like herself is likely to make only twenty dollars a month and has to grow a garden just to feed the family, if not work a second job as well. Everything moves slowly and torturously.

But here's my point: Life isn't easy in the U.S. either. And that isn't as obvious. It simply isn't easy being part of the "First World." Though we are privileged, we are likely to feel trapped. Trapped inside a set of different, invisible restraints.

Actually, though Vi probably does belong in Uganda, only a few are truly called to that other world, and I don't think I am one of them, at least not right now. So the question for me is this: How can I live gracefully in my own realm, no matter how confining and spiritually empty it seems? Better yet, how can I redeem that realm? How can all of us who live in the "First World" bring new life to our settings, whether we live in Canada or Australia or Singapore? Whether we have a home in London or Hong Kong or a wealthy neighborhood of Rio de Janeiro?

The only solution I can see is for us to transform our society into a part of the kingdom that Jesus proclaimed. And that means living out a radically different Christianity, a Christianity that doesn't conform.

On Earth As in Heaven

The problem with trying to be a good "American Christian" is that I can confuse being American with being Christian. I can be like the little girl who wrote, with a child's spelling, in a letter to God, "Dear God, I am Amearican. What are you?"[1]

God's kingdom is too wide open and liberated to be squeezed into America, no matter how big it is. The kingdom won't fit into what I call a "democratic state." And it definitely won't fit into a single denomination, let alone one church building.

In that sense, contextualizing the gospel means confronting my context, not adapting to it. If I feel spiritually imprisoned, then I need to ask Christ's help to recognize what is imprisoning me. And what is the freedom that Jesus offers? After all, he came to free us. He said, "If you hold to my teaching, you are really my disciples. Then you will know the truth, and the truth will set you free" (Jn 8:31-32).

Apparently, becoming free spiritually begins with simply holding to Jesus' teaching—being a disciple. When we do this we claim him as King, and the kingdom grows. What better starting place for this process than the church? But before we can start we need a radical new experience of church, because often it is not representative of the kingdom.

From what Jesus taught, I gather that the church is not the building we worship in or the form of worship we are accustomed to. The structures we choose for worship are no more important than the structures of Judaism that Jesus confronted when he brought the gospel to Israel. Over and over he challenged the Pharisees and Sadducees, deriding them for their love of ceremony and status and long prayers and rules. "You blind guides!" he said, "You strain out a gnat but swallow a camel" (Mt 23:24).

I used to applaud when reading such passages. Then I felt the camel kicking in my own throat: *What if I am the modern-day equivalent of a Pharisee? After all, I am a second-generation Christian, carefully raised in the evangelical church, schooled to know the rules and to follow them religiously. And yet I have struggled a lot with spiritual dryness.*

In reality, when I have felt renewed, it usually wasn't in a church, at least not as I think of it traditionally. For instance, one of my best "church" experiences was in a fellowship of Christians that I've mentioned before: the Wellspring fellowship, which formed spontaneously in Manhattan, Kansas.

A New Model

Wellspring, when it sprang up in 1983, began because people were going to their own churches each Sunday but not finding spiritual satisfaction. A simple discussion group started, meeting to talk about what it meant to be a Christian, but this grew into much more: family conferences, spiritual dynamics conferences, a ministry to international students, an annual Easter sunrise service, a Christmas program, a traditional Jewish *seder* service and more.

Over the last ten years, Wellspring has had all sorts of activities, but the hallmark of the group has been spiritual fellowship, free and open fellowship. People have gathered not out of obligation but out of a desire to be together. Anyone was welcome. And there has always been a Spirit-led flexibility for trying something new. People at Wellspring simply want to know how to be like Christ, then to do it.

Seven years after Wellspring began, one of the first members looked back at its history. She identified a number of key freedoms:
☐ freedom to discover one's unique gifts
☐ freedom to use gifts
☐ freedom to experiment and grow
☐ freedom to be with people from different backgrounds
☐ freedom to develop deep relationships
☐ freedom to receive personal attention
☐ freedom to be (not just do)
☐ freedom to act on a vision, releasing creative energy
Indeed the truth was setting them free!

The Church Redefined

Over the years Wellspring members have asked, "Should we become a church?" And every time they have answered their own question with a firm no.

For me the question is amusing because, whether they want to be or not, they *are* the church. They may not meet in a church building, but they are definitely part of *the* church. Yes, I emphasize *the,* because *the* church, spanning all the continents and centuries, is much larger and freer than *a* church. And as Christians our allegiance to *the* church is more important than our allegiance to *a* church. Only if we are busy contributing to *the* church will we really be able to contribute to *a* church. That's the kingdom that we are trying to build—on earth as in heaven—and that's the kingdom of which Wellspring is a part.

Sadly enough, today the traditional concept of churches has become so rigid and confining that it has cut people off from this larger, growing body of Christ. It has squashed the hopes of many who sincerely wanted to grow spiritually. Thus the same woman who described the freedoms of Wellspring also wrote,

If Wellspring did become a church, somebody would:

capture it—not "ours" anymore

dominate it—not "everybody's"

throttle it—not free

separate it—not familyish

sterilize it—not creative

codify it—not open doctrinally

limit it—not allow anyone in

expand it—not a small group anymore

clergify it—not lay led

bore it—not fun

exhaust it—not sensitive to people's gifts

Sundayify it—not real to life

What a sad commentary on churches, if indeed many of them are experienced this way. They don't have to be like that.

Pharisees Not Needed

To Jesus, achieving Christian community was pretty simple: "For where two or three come together in my name, there am I with them" (Mt 18:20). Being his faithful disciple was more fundamental than being part of a certain group: Baptist or Presbyterian, evangelical or ecumenical, Pharisee or Sadducee.

Of course, all of us who attend a church in a particular denomination are helped in certain ways. I must admit I do have some strong memories of stained glass, particularly from a chapel at the University of Kansas where, with just the right angle of sunlight, each morning the red glass would glow like blood against a dark blue background, in such brilliant contrast that it made me meditate on the blood of Christ, so precious, so priceless, so horridly beautiful.

For me, seeing is vital, so I am not surprised that such a visual memory is important. For another person from another denomination, something else might stick: a certain style of music, the sermons of a certain minister, receiving Communion. These all affect our decision about which local church we will attend. But if we were to strip them away, the thing that would remain, defining *the* one true church, would be a group of people with a worshipful and loving commitment to Jesus.

In that sense, the church can't be defined by or contained in a building, or a minister, or a prayer book, or a choir. It is a vibrant, ever-growing group of people who share a desire to be like Christ, to do everything in accordance with Christ's will. With these wonderful disciples, whether on a Sunday morning or a Tuesday afternoon, whether at coffee hour or eating dinner, whether at the Communion rail or bicycling, we will always find meaning and purpose and pleasure.

Jesus came not to destroy organized religion, but to fulfill it. Thus he exclaimed to a Samaritan, who had her own concept of what was truly religious, "Believe me, woman, a time is coming when you will worship the Father neither on this mountain nor in Jerusalem. . . . A time is coming and has now come when the true worshipers will worship the Father in spirit and truth, for they are the kind of worshipers the Father seeks" (Jn 4:21-23).

With Jesus' resurrection and the coming of the Holy Spirit, we can experience worship in spirit and in truth. We can now even experience it in our local churches—if we are open to God's larger plan and purposes, and if we work at being Christlike, not Presbyterian or Pentecostal or Episcopalian.

Bridging the Denominational Gap

As a former member of an independent Baptist church, I have my pet peeves. How is it that such a small Protestant church could get the notion that it fully represents the Christian faith without being connected to the traditions of the past? Some members even acted as if Christianity didn't get invented until Luther, when in fact virtually the only way to be Christian from Christ to Luther was to be Catholic—either Roman Catholic or Eastern Orthodox.

The Nicene Creed, the Apostles' Creed, the liturgical year (with its symbolism of Christ's life, death and resurrection)—all of these were developed in the Catholic church. St. Augustine, St. Francis, St. Teresa of Avila, St. Thomas à Kempis, St. Julian of Norwich, St. John of the Cross—all of these wonderful Christians were devout members of the Catholic church. The very books of the Bible were canonized by members of that Catholic church. And yet people in this little "independent" church that I attended, two thousand years removed from the early church, often operated as if a single minister (with the help of a few appointed elders) could capture and fully interpret the kingdom of God, ignoring all the developments of the past.

Every denomination runs a similar risk. Now that I attend the Episcopal church, I have been introduced to liturgical worship. *The Book of Common Prayer* is its centerpiece, and I have met some Episcopalians who act as if they can't reach God without the *Book of Common Prayer* opened to just the right page.

Though beautifully written and based solidly on the Bible, this book cannot replace either the Bible or honest, direct prayer. A prayer book is a tool, not a law. And like the sabbath, it was made for us, not us for it. In the end, the danger of this reliance on past traditions is that it can seduce the individual into a false sense of personal security. If one simply belongs to an Episcopal church, everything is okay.

Either way it is easy to fall. "It is always simple to fall," said G. K. Chesterton; "there are an infinity of angles at which one falls, only one at which one stands."[2]

We need balance, if we want to stay standing. There is so much we can learn from each other, in our various denominations and traditions. On the positive side, Baptists have a firm grasp of the importance of personal commitment. They know that no ritual is more important than the basic relationship between an individual and God. Episcopalians, on the other hand, see the importance of the community and of history. They know that any one person trying to understand God by himself or herself is incomplete.

Put these two views together and a Christian is not likely to fall in either direction—by creating some peculiar personal brand of Christianity and forcing it on others, or by assuming personal salvation simply because he or she was baptized as an infant and raised in "a Christian home." Put the two views together and a Christian is even more likely to be like Christ. So we need to be talking to each other. Even if it involves arguing!

Something Big—*Really* Big

But if we can learn so much crossculturally among these little subcultures, without ever leaving our homes, how much more, then, could be ours as Christians if only we would open ourselves to the kingdom outside our national boundaries. How much more is available to Christians in any country, if they are open to the Christians elsewhere!

Since the kingdom is much larger than any nation, it needs to be seen as a global reality, connecting all continents and all people. The kingdom didn't fit inside Israel, so it broke loose, spilling into Samaria, Greece, Rome, Africa, and eventually Spain, England, Latin America, Asia, the United States.

The kingdom still can't be contained. No country owns Christianity. We who belong to Christ are part of something much larger, more wonderfully open and free. Not even the earth is large enough for this reality. Christ's kingdom spills out billions of light years into outer space and still isn't contained, for its subjects are not limited to physical reality as we know it.

The kingdom isn't complete without those who lived before and those still to come. The kingdom must include past and present and future. So we who are building the kingdom on earth at this time are connected with all of history and all of reality—with heaven itself. We are part of something so vast and glorious that it makes our governments, our religious structures, our way of doing things in one particular country at one particular time almost insignificant. We are not insignificant, though, because we are still part of the whole. But we are definitely small. And that is why for us to know the fullness of the kingdom we must know churches outside our own church. We need *the* church in all its forms.

Eyes of an Outsider

To fully appreciate the size and momentum of the kingdom of God, I must listen to Christians outside my society. I need to do this, if for no other reason, because building the kingdom means creating an alternative lifestyle. By myself, I am too close to my culture to recognize its assumed values and separate them from the gospel message. But in relation to the church worldwide, I can see myself finally with the eyes of the outsider, the one who knows another life. Then I can distinguish what is Christian from what is merely cultural.

Father Vincent Donovan, an American missionary who took the gospel to the Masai of East Africa, later returned to minister in Chicago. When he came back, he saw the U.S. with the eyes of a Masai. He explained that sometimes Christians in one country are like people who have been at a party too long. They don't recognize the odors in the room—until they step out. Then, when they come back, they can smell the cigarette smoke, the twice-breathed musty air, the liquor, the sweat.[3]

Over and over, I've been helped to smell American culture invading my Christan life by hearing from others who have stepped into the U.S. from outside. For example, Peter Kusmic, from Yugoslavia, who said, a few years after he had finished graduate studies in the U.S.:

"There are so many things in America; thank God we don't need them. . . . I never saw a mall while I was in America; I didn't need it."[4]

Or there is Isaac Phiri, from Zambia, who exclaimed, "In the U.S., evangelists say, 'You are not the center of your life; God is.' That was never the problem for me growing up in Africa because I was raised to know that I was not the center of the universe. The question was, *Who should be at the center?*"[5]

Ajith Fernando, from Sri Lanka, insisted at a conference: "People in this culture have lost the value of suffering." Then he went on to explain that the consequence is low commitment. When anything causes too much difficulty Americans simply drop it, because they don't see the value of suffering—the discipline and character that it forms, as well as the community support that develops.[6]

Or what about the elderly Romanian gentleman who said, "What began in Judea as faith in a man became in Greece a philosophy, in Rome an institution, in Europe a culture, and in the USA a business."

Neither Greek Nor Jew

Fortunately, being able to see ourselves from the outside doesn't just lead to self-criticism. It also leads to appreciation.

One of the delights of returning to America from the outside is that at last I am able to see our strengths—our cultural beauty. Often friends overseas help me to see those strengths—to smell the good as well as the bad. Now, when I fly back to the United States, there are a host of American qualities that I look forward to. I look forward to fast and friendly service, convenience, frank conversation, optimism, fairness, tolerance, a wonderful openness of movement and activity. I look forward, in essence, to personal freedom.

Being American, with all of its inherent problems, is a gift, and the worst thing I can do is take it for granted. Indeed, I am fortunate to live in such a society. I should thank God daily for the privilege. And I need not go around constantly apologizing for my "Americanness." Christians from other cultures are not somehow better; they are only different. They represent some Christlike reality that I need. But, thank God, we Americans also represent something they need. Without all of us, the body of Christ is not complete.

That's why I keep traveling overseas to coach Christian writers. Not just because I want to give to those with less, but because I want to receive from those with more. I am convinced that all God's people are equally gifted and that we suffer when the communication goes only one way, from the economically privileged to the needy. And so I train other writers in hopes that they will strengthen their voices—strengthen them until we can hear them clear across oceans, bursting through all boundaries of nationality and denomination.

Christians in Sudan should not have to feel "dependent." Neither should American Christians have to feel "independent." Jesus freed us from those roles when he asked us to love one another. He called us instead to be *interdependent*, always sharing with each other. That is why the new church lived in open community, sharing equally. With the help of the Holy Spirit at Pentecost, they were freed from their Jewish culture and could reach out to include everyone from every culture. Suddenly they spoke in all languages, breaking the barriers that had existed ever since the Tower of Babel. Something revolutionary happened, and they were able to turn back the cultural splintering of centuries, with all the horrors of domination that went with it. They became unified in their diversity, unified as members of the same kingdom, Christ's kingdom. They became free of all the old limitations of color and wealth and sex and status. In essence they became *the* church, the ever-growing, irrepressible body of Christ.

That's the kingdom we belong to, and we damage it when we cling to our own brand of Christianity or force it on others. We trap ourselves in a tiny space when instead all of creation, both earth and heaven, could be our territory.

A Sense of Belonging

In closing, I return to where I began: my own spiritual birthplace, the African nation of Ethiopia.

Before the Marxist revolution in Ethiopia, the leaders of Messerete Hiwot Church thought they had a large building. Fifteen years later, with persecution still going on and Christians imprisoned for their faith, the building was too small. They couldn't fit everyone in.

Returning to Ethiopia on a visit with Cathy, I was privileged one Sunday to go to the first of their three services, at 6:30 a.m. We arrived at 6:00 to get a seat, and even then the church was nearly full. The people were kneeling on the floor, turned toward the back of the church and bowed over their pews. The building rumbled with murmured prayers.

As we sat there, people kept coming in, out of the chilled gray air. At the gate we had met a legless man who drove a three-wheeled motorcycle. He came in from a side door, on his hands, swinging his torso across the floor. Then he lifted himself onto the edge of the front platform and perched there to see. *What private woes is he carrying?* I wondered. And yet he seemed so confident and at ease.

The church filled, yet still they came. Some filed quietly out a side door and found seating in an open tin-roofed shed. I could see them praying out there, beyond the haze of eucalyptus smoke that rolled in from neighboring cooking fires, sharp-scented as incense.

With a few minutes to go, a church leader asked everyone to stand. Then he asked for four from the congregation to lead in public prayers.

What prayers these were! Chanting, rolling prayers that built and built, crescendoing into loud corporate amens. I couldn't understand a word, but still I felt I was part of it. I prayed along, hearing soft prayers all around me. Then, after each of the four had taken his turn and the murmuring voices had died down, the service began.

There were hymns, then more praying, and a sermon. But the most striking element in the service was the choir.

How can one describe such music? It lifted and fell and rolled along. It seemed gentle and warm and full of feeling. Above all, it seemed shaped for praise.

They sang softly, accompanied by a simple guitar and an accordion; and as they sang—shifting their weight from foot to foot and staring out over the heads of the congregation, out through the roof into heaven itself—I wept. I noticed others wept too: an old businessman with a peppery beard who held his face in his hands, and a younger man who wiped his eyes with a handkerchief.

I looked up again, to a woman who sang at one end of the choir, her face lifted exultantly, beatific with peace and hope. I was entranced.

At points the sharp trill of ululation would rise out of the congregation, uttered by someone who was overcome. Over the lilting lyrics we could hear these trills, full of pain and triumph, full of praise. They rose like a challenge, pushing back the night and all its suffering and terror, bringing hope and purpose and meaning where there had been none.

Then it was over.

Our host explained as we filed out of the church that on the previous day a member of the choir had committed suicide, overcome at last with the difficulty of life in communist Ethiopia, wartorn and impoverished Ethiopia. He hardly had to tell me. That grief had been there in the music. Even without knowing the words, I had heard it. But I had also been comforted in ways I could not understand. The Spirit had interceded for us all, as Paul put in in his letter to the Romans, "with groans that words cannot express" (Rom 8:26).

What happened to me at that church service was bigger than the choir or the unique setting. Members of the congregation had their own problems to deal with, no doubt, just as in any other church. But I could tell that they were worshiping in spirit and in truth, as Jesus predicted to the Samaritan woman so long ago. The same Holy Spirit who breathed into the church at Pentecost, bringing it to life, was breathing into them. The same church that was growing in their midst was growing in my midst. I belonged with them despite the different languages, despite the different ways of singing and praying.

There is nothing more powerful for me than experiencing that sense of belonging, often where I least expect it, among strangers in a strange place. We, together, as Christians, are part of something larger than Messerete Hiwot Church or my home church or *any* church. We are part of the biggest and most wonderful community that exists—the kingdom of God. And that makes the world a family.

* * *

There is always more to explore and more to say. But I hope I have at least begun to answer my own question: *If I'm so free as an American Christian, why do I feel so trapped?* When it comes down to it, maybe I don't have to feel trapped. Swimming against the tide of my culture, in solidarity with Christians who are swimming against the tide elsewhere, I begin to get a glimpse of something that has always been real, just hard to see. I am *free.* In Christ, I am free to live differently. I am not limited to the way of life my culture offers.

I'm a member of Christ's society. I am not limited to that little clan called "family," who share a last name and the same ways of doing things. I am not limited to the larger tribe of the college-educated middle class, or to the group called men, or to the Episcopalians. Above all, I am not limited to being American. I am Christian, and that is better, because as a Christian I am free of all labels and restraints. Jesus sets me free from even the limits I place on myself. He makes me part of something wonderfully big and open. All I have to do is say, "Lord, I am yours." Then, ironically, I am free to be myself, my *true* self. God is good indeed!

Notes

Chapter 2: Prisoners of Freedom

[1]Associated Press, "Lawn chair helps fulfill dream of soaring in sky," *Topeka Capital-Journal,* Sunday, July 4, 1982, p. 41.

[2]Ralph Waldo Emerson, *Self Reliance,* published in *The Norton Anthology of American Literature,* 2 vols., ed. Ronald Gottesman et al. (New York: W. W. Norton, 1979), 1:723-743.

[3]Bharati Mukherjhee, interview, *Bill Moyers: A World of Ideas,* 2 vols., ed. Andie Tucher (New York: Doubleday, 1990), 2:3.

[4]Alvin Toffler, *Future Shock* (New York: Bantam, 1971), pp. 291-96 and 318.

Chapter 4: Escape from Myself

[1]Thomas Jefferson, "The Declaration of Independence," in *The Norton Anthology of American Literature,* 2 vols. ed. Ronald Gottesman et al. (New York: W. W. Norton, 1979), 1:495.

[2]Benjamin Franklin, "The Way to Wealth," in *The Norton Anthology of American Literature,* 2 vols., ed. Ronald Gottesman et al. (New York: W. W. Norton, 1979), 1:267.

[3]Robert N. Bellah, Richard Madsen, William M. Sullivan, Ann Swidler and Steven M. Tipton, *Habits of the Heart* (New York: Harper & Row, 1986), p. 37.

[4]Bruce Springsteen, "Born to Run," *Born to Run,* Columbia, PC 33795, 1975.

[5]Ibid.

[6]Garrison Keillor, "Letter from Jim," *News from Lake Wobegon: Spring,* Minnesota Public Radio, PHC 909, 1983.

Chapter 5: Released to Risk

[1]David Gilmour and Roger Waters, "Comfortably Numb?" from *Pink Floyd: The Wall*

(London: Pink Floyd Music Publishers, Ltd., 1980), p. 79.

[2]Aleksandr Solzhenitsyn, *The Gulag Archipelago: An Experiment in Literary Investigation III-IV,* trans. Thomas P. Whitney (New York: Harper & Row, 1975), p. 613.

[3]Wallace Shawn and Andre Gregory, *My Dinner With Andre* (New York: Grove Press, 1981), pp. 76-77.

[4]Thomas à Kempis, *Of the Imitation of Christ* (Grand Rapids: Baker Book House, 1973), p. 106.

Chapter 6: Truth Set Loose
[1]David Byrne, "Road to Nowhere," *Little Creatures,* by Talking Heads, Sire Records Company, 1-25305, 1985.

[2]Allan Bloom, *The Closing of the American Mind* (New York: Simon and Schuster, 1987), p. 27.

Chapter 7: Out of Our Minds
[1]Carl Gustav Jung, *Psychology and Religion* (New Haven, Conn.: Yale University Press, 1938), p. 16.

[2]Ibid.

[3]C. S. Lewis, *The Screwtape Letters* (London: Geoffrey Bles: The Centenary Press, 1942), p. 39.

[4]Karl Marx, *Karl Marx: Early Writings,* trans. T. B. Bottomore (New York: McGraw-Hill, 1963), pp. 43-44.

[5]Robert H. Schuller, *The Be (Happy) Attitudes* (New York: Bantam, 1987), p. 16.

[6]Alcoholics Anonymous World Services, Inc., *Alcoholics Anonymous,* 3rd ed. (New York: Alcoholics Anonymous World Services, Inc., 1976), p. 59.

Chapter 9: Rescued from Success
[1]John Winthrop, "A Model of Christian Charity," *Norton Anthology of American Literature,* 2 vols., ed. Ronald Gottesman et al. (New York: W.W. Norton and Company, 1979), 1:24.

[2]Ibid., 1:23.

[3]Priscilla Painton, "The Taming of Ted Turner," *Time,* January 6, 1992, pp. 34-36.

[4]*The Book of Common Prayer,* According to the Use of the Episcopal Church (New York: The Seabury Press, 1979), p. 358.

[5]Winthrop, "A Model of Christian Charity," 1:19.

Chapter 13: Back to Nature
[1]Greg Brown, "Canned Goods," *One More Goodnight Kiss,* Red House Records, RHR 23, 1988.

Chapter 14: Liberty for All
[1]*Children's Letters to God,* compiled by Stuart Hample and Eric Marshall (New York:

Workman Publishing, 1991).

[2]G. K. Chesterton, *Orthodoxy* (New York: Doubleday/Image, 1990), p. 101.

[3]Vincent J. Donovan, *The Church in the Midst of Creation* (Maryknoll, N.Y.: Orbis Books, 1989), p. 126.

[4]Spoken at an Urbana convention; used by permission.

[5]Spoken at a Litt-World convention; used by permission.

[6]Spoken at an Urbana convention; used by permission.